D1292321

# ECONOMICS and
# The Art of Controversy

# THE 1954

# BROWN & HALEY LECTURES

*are the second of a series given annually at the
College of Puget Sound, Tacoma, Washington
by a scholar distinguished for his work
in Social Studies or the Humanities
The purpose of these Lectures is to
present an original analysis of
some intellectual problems
confronting the present age*

# ECONOMICS

# &

# *The Art of Controversy*

John Kenneth Galbraith

1955

**RUTGERS UNIVERSITY PRESS**

NEW BRUNSWICK • NEW JERSEY

For ALAN

# Preface

SHOULD this essay, by some mischance, fall into the hands of obtuse or evil persons, it could easily be misconstrued. Such persons could have me insisting that all economic debate has now come to an end and that a reign of sweetness has replaced the bickering, nose-punching, and occasional eviscerations of another day. Nothing could be farther from my meaning. The capacity of economics to provoke argument seems to me still strong. No doubt there will be as much controversy over economic questions in the future as in the past, and economists should find this encouraging, for much of their income, as well as most of their prestige, derives from the persistent tendency of people to get exercised over this subject.

If there is some serious economic misfortune in the near future—for example, a disagreeable depression—the argument over what to do, and how much, and when to do it will probably become quite uncouth. This will be certain if anyone comes up with a new idea on depression therapy. As it happens, there have been no new ideas on this subject now for nearly twenty years.

The argument of these pages, rather, is that the

present topics of economic controversy have seen their best days. Even this does not mean that there has been any diminution in the noise of battle. Where the art of controversy is well developed, as with us, a very small amount of substance will sustain a very great deal of fury. My case is only that the substance back of most of our current economic arguments is, indeed, rather slight. On some subjects it has become hard to think of anything new to say. As a widely regarded philosopher of our economic system remarked not long ago, "Our present need is for some new platitudes." But there is every assurance that we shall continue to unleash the old platitudes with undiminished vigor. There is also a chance—no one should wish it—that some wholly new issue will appear to arouse our passions. Those who have learned to love that most nostalgic of all the sounds of *our* countryside, that of outraged conservatives baying for the blood of an economic heretic, should not feel distressed.

This small book first took form as a series of lectures at the College of Puget Sound in Tacoma, Washington, in the spring of 1954. I remain in the debt of many people on that verdant and lovely shore. President R. Franklin Thompson of the College of Puget Sound was my distinguished and attentive host. Professor Lyle S. Shelmidine, the able historian who first organized the lecture series, spared no effort to make my visit memorable. President Fred T. Haley of the Brown & Haley Company, the sponsor of the lectures, along with all the other members of a notably incisive and gracious family, sought me out to discuss nearly every point I made. No lecturer is ever paid a higher compliment. I must also say a word of thanks to the students, trustees, and townspeople who sat through the lectures. This essay tells of our joy, as a people, in fighting over economic questions. No one ever suggested that we have any similar pleasure in listening silently to a lecture on the subject.

JOHN KENNETH GALBRAITH

*Cambridge, Massachusetts*
*October 1954*

# Contents

# ECONOMICS and
# The Art of Controversy

# O N E

# Sound and Substance

AMONG the peoples of the world we of the United States undoubtedly have a certain reputation for the violence of the language in which we conduct the public business. The character and motives of our public figures are regularly praised or maligned in terms that are not remarkable for their restraint. And we are rarely given either to doubt or modesty in ascribing consequences to particular public measures or actions. They promise either the millenium or disaster, and the most telling argument is normally made by the man who is at once the most dogmatic in saying what will happen and the most imaginative in picturing the details.

It would probably be a mistake to suppose that the violence of our debate is a measure of our national vigor. To be able to make a point intelligently, persuasively, and quietly may well be a mark of strength. Wild insults, loud denunciations, and ridiculous exaggeration are an indication of inadequacy not only in everyday citizens but also in senators. There is no reason for democracy to partake of the nature of a barroom brawl. However, the purpose of this essay is not to suggest an improvement in public manners or in the comportment of our debate on public issues. Such suggestions have been made before without notable effect. Rather its purpose is to look beyond the sound and fury of contemporary political argument in one important field of affairs—that having to do with economic policy—and to see how grave are the questions being debated. It is always possible that a cool and tolerably unemotional examination of issues will serve as an antidote to the more commonplace exaggeration and overstatement. If this should lead, in turn, to some mellowing of our behavior in public debate, this would be a pleasant by-product. We can remember with hope Swift's suggestion: "As the best law is founded upon reason, so are the best manners."

It is no part of my purpose to seek for agreement where none exists. This, paradoxically, is another bad habit of the time. Just as political leaders, publicists, and pundits regularly, if metaphorically, bloody each other's noses over issues that are more synthetic than real, there are other occasions when they find it desirable to proclaim their complete harmony or, at least, the vastness of their area of agreement, to a world which knows, or should know, that the disagreement is nearly total. The consequences of disguising disagreement are likely, in the end, to be as disenchanting as those of exaggerating it. Like dust, disagreement can be swept under the rug but, unlike dust, it will not stay there. It will be recalled that in the spring of 1954, a few days before the row between Secretary of the Army Robert T. Stevens and Senator Joseph R. McCarthy went into its climactic phase, the two met over a chicken luncheon and, ostensibly, settled all of their differences.

This essay is almost entirely concerned with economic controversy. Economic questions, which must be taken to include those involving economic power, have been the major subject of dispute over most of our national history. It is true that on occasion moral questions (the inherent rights and wrongs of slavery, or whether a man's responsibility as his brother's keeper should encompass his brother's sobriety) have agitated us rather deeply. At the moment we are having an impassioned argument over the constitutional rights and immunities of the individual. Yet, year in and year out, it is the questions of economics—the manifold issues surrounding collective bargaining, the problems of farm price policy, tariffs, public spending, taxation, and the regulation of business—which provide us with the bread and butter of political controversy. It is these that give us our daily diet of insinuation, indignation, and insult. As a people, we react violently to the suggestion that we are materialistic. Certainly we are not. But in searching for the reasons for the long-standing preeminence of economic issues as objects of political controversy, it is perhaps fair to say that we are intelligently sensitive to political activity in the vicinity of our pocketbooks.

## II

In citing evidence of agreement and disagreement, I shall have occasion to refer to the economic positions that are proclaimed by various organizations: the business organizations, the trade unions, and the farm organizations. I shall also have something to say about the economic platforms and programs of political parties.

For many, it is an axiom that the organizations I mention do not really represent their members. And impressive evidence can be adduced in proof of the point. A few years ago, *Fortune* magazine found from a rough sample of the membership of the National Association of Manufacturers that a majority of businessmen took strong and frequently profane exception to the official doctrines of their organization.[1] As this is written, the American Farm Bureau Federation, the largest and most influential of the farm organizations, is endeavoring to persuade Congress to accept so-called flexible, as distinct from fixed or rigid, price supports for farm products. It is as certain as any such matter can be that a free vote by the members of the bureau would register a substantial majority in favor of the position which the leaders are opposing. To those who, at least in their own view, know the workingman best it has long been obvi-

[1] William H. Whyte, Jr. and editors of *Fortune, Is Anybody Listening*. New York: Simon and Schuster, 1952.

ous that he is the unwilling captive of his union leaders, although it is not certain that the worker has ever felt his peonage as acutely as have his non-laboring friends. The political parties, in the common view, are perhaps the most egregiously unrepresentative organizations of all. The traditional and conservative Democratic rank and file of the South and their friends elsewhere are led by a few aggressive northern radicals. The great Republican party, which owes so much to the pre-Cambrian leaders of the Midwest, has been captured and subverted by eastern internationalists and "me-tooer's."

Some of these divergences between leaders and followers are important. I shall deal at length with one of them in the final chapter. However, the faithfulness with which leaders mirror the attitudes and aspirations of their followers is not a prime issue here. The concern of this book is with agreement and disagreement not as it involves people at large, but as it manifests itself in political positions that are taken and defended. It is the leaders who take the positions and do the defending. Accordingly, they are the people who are of interest here. In looking at a battle wherein words are the weapons there is no need to be concerned with the inarticulate and hence the unarmed.

The next five chapters survey the current state of controversy on four matters that, in recent times, have been subjects of urgent debate. These, in order, are labor, farm policy, the larger issues of government responsibility for the performance of the economy, and the question of the Welfare State. The final chapter looks into some of the consequences of the present state of agreement and dissent.

# TWO

# A Question of Coexistence

THE most serious friction that can arise between
two persons occurs when one denies the right
of the other to exist. The same is so between
groups. It is in such a denial of the right to exist
that the classic capitalist dispute—that between
trade unions and private employers—has its ori-
gins. Employers anciently denied the right of
existence to unions. Accordingly, the argument
was bitter. It is evident that when the principle
of coexistence is conceded by both groups, the
nature of the dispute is fundamentally altered.

These far from obscure propositions are ex-
tremely important for understanding the controversy which from day to day and year to year
characterizes the phenomenon which, in the
United States, we call collective bargaining. Until
comparatively recent times, the right of existence
of one interest in the labor market was strenuously denied by another. In 1903 the position of
employers on unions was stated with considerable
clarity by the then recently organized National
Association of Manufacturers as follows:

"Organized labor knows but one law, and that is the law of physical force—the law of the Huns and the Vandals, the law of the savage. All its purposes are accomplished by either the actual force or the threat of force. . . . It is, in all essential features, a mob power, knowing no master except its own free will."[1]

This was a fair reflection of current employer attitudes. It was only a few months before that George F. Baer (one of the anthracite operators then involved in the great coal strike) achieved his accidental immortality with the declaration that "The rights and interests of the laboring man will be protected and cared for, not by labor agitators, but by the Christian men to whom God in His infinite wisdom has given the control of the property interests of the country."[2] Such amiable expressions imply no disposition to tolerate unions, and, in fact, there was no such disposition for many years to come. As late as 1935 the leading historians of American trade unionism observed:

"To the American labor movement the conquest of the right to exist was ever its paramount problem. English employers had with few excep-

[1] Alfred Cleveland, *Some Political Aspects of Organized Industry*. Unpublished thesis, Harvard University, October 1946.

[2] Selig Perlman and Philip Taft, *History of Labor in the United States, 1896-1932*. New York: Macmillan, 1953, p. 43. (This is also quoted by Frederick Lewis Allen in *The Great Pierpont Morgan*. New York: Harper, 1949, p. 224.)

tions accepted unionism before the end of the Nineteenth Century. . . . But to American employers unionism has always remained the invader and the usurper to be expelled at the first opportunity."[3]

It would add greatly to the symmetry of the discussion if, while employers denied to unions the right to existence, employees had also denied the right of employers to exist. This is the practical effect of a socialist (or anarchist or syndicalist) working class movement. In principle, although hardly in practice, it is also the position of the traditionally socialist labor movements of Western Europe.[4] However, the American union did not in general reciprocate the lethal aims and ambitions of the employers. At the turn of the century Daniel DeLeon sought to promote a socialist trade union movement, but the effort was largely in vain. The International Workers of the World in the years following was rather erratically anticapitalist. But the American Federation of Labor, the main custodian of the labor tradition, remained staunchly antisocialist. "The fact that socialism is

[3] Perlman and Taft, p. 621.

[4] Although private employers in Western Europe (excluding Spain and Portugal, and Germany and Italy during the Nazi-Fascist period) have long taken unions more or less for granted, the ideology of the worker does not normally return the compliment. In the United States, by contrast, it is the right of existence of the union that has been denied, while workers have taken the private employer for granted.

not only impracticable, but a crude and undeveloped theory is becoming more manifest every day," the federation asserted firmly in 1901, adding that "the socialists before they try to reform the world should reform themselves." There is little indication that the AF of L's unwanted offspring, the CIO, was ever more effectively socialist in its tendencies than its parent. It is doubtful if even the Communist-dominated unions, when they existed, leaned very heavily on the idea that private employers would soon disappear in the United States.

Although it takes two to make a quarrel, one person can cause considerable disturbance if he is sufficiently bent on destroying someone else. Labor's effort to exist was certain to be a cause of bitter trouble as long as that right was denied as a matter of principle by employers. Since the right was denied, we long ago came to expect that disputes in the labor market would be impassioned and exhibit a tendency to descend into violence and bloodshed.

This was the old precondition to argument in the labor market. However, it is one that no longer holds. The right of the union to exist is now generally granted. There are, to be sure, industries and regions (the latter most notably in the South) where this is not so. But over the great part of the American economy the union is accepted. Few corporation presidents today remember, as a matter of personal experience, the days when they had no union to deal with.

The transition of American capitalism from a largely unorganized to a predominantly organized labor market was one of the spectacular changes of that great decade of change, the thirties. A variety of factors—the fact that time had caught up with the United States, the NRA, the Wagner Act, the generally benign attitude of the New Deal toward unions, and the energetic (and also exceedingly courageous) leadership that appeared in the labor movement at the time—all played a part. Although the change had many facets and was in full movement for several years, it is a shame not to recognize a particular date which all historians will count of special importance. That was March 3, 1937, when Myron C. Taylor and John L. Lewis announced their agreement on recognition of the Steel Workers Organizing Committee of the CIO by the plants of the United States Steel Corporation. Prior to that time, the union was a fact of life in many industries. In some it was regarded as inevitable; in a good many more it was regarded as a misfortune. But there were few employers who regarded unions as part of the natural order of things, and there were many who cherished the hope that they might one day be relieved of the incubus. With the acceptance of the CIO by the United States Steel Corporation, labor was en-

trenched in the heartland of heavy industry. Moreover, the steel industry in general, and the
corporation in particular, had been the center of
the resistance to unions and the source of some of
labor's classic reverses. It was at the Homestead
Works of the predecessor Carnegie Steel Company
in 1892 that the pioneer National Amalgamated
Association of Iron and Steel Workers struck for
143 days, and it was there, on July 6 of that year,
that seven men were killed and three times that
number wounded in a battle with the Pinkertons.
That strike was lost, and labor lost again and
disastrously to the corporation in 1901, 1910, and
1919. In 1919, Judge Gary coolly summarized the
policy of the corporation: It "does not confer, ne-
gotiate, or combat labor unions as such."[5]

## II

During the fifteen years that followed the peace
pact of the Mayflower Hotel—an agreement to be
sure which some continued to regard as the historic
betrayal by the nation's classic capitalist to its most
obnoxious labor leader—there were far more labor
disputes than in the fifteen years or possibly even
in the fifty years preceding. More billingsgate was
unleashed in the political debate over labor relations. More people were also involved in that
debate. During the war, on occasion, John L.

5 Perlman and Taft, p. 463.

Lewis all but crowded Hitler from the headlines, and there were some, undoubtedly, who regarded him as the greater threat to our way of life. After the war came the Taft-Hartley Act and the inspired union phrases about "the slave labor law" and "legalized union busting."

The argument over Taft-Hartley continues. So do strikes. The crimes of the labor bosses are still celebrated in the writs of Mr. Westbrook Pegler. And not all employers are reconciled to unions. At the last meeting of the National Association of Manufacturers a keynote speaker was assigned the indubitably significant task of identifying the barriers to a "growing America." After breathing deeply, he listed among the obstacles "The growth of monopolistic control over the jobs of the American people with its depressing effects on productivity and its use by so-called labor leaders to promote socialistic and totalitarian political ideology." He called on his fellow employers for an "intelligent and courageous" assault on unions whose activities constitute an "unjust infringement of American workers' individual liberty."[6]

Yet it is precisely this continuing (though undoubtedly diminishing) dispute over labor rela-

[6] "Barriers to a Growing America." Address by John T. Brown, President, J. I. Case Co., at the 58th Session of The Annual Congress of Industry, National Association of Manufacturers, New York City, December 2, 1953. New York: National Association of Manufacturers, 1953.

tions which teaches us the first lesson about economic controversy. The noise and the violence and imaginativeness of the invective are no measure whatever of the importance of the issue. (Later I shall show in fact that the correlation is more likely inverse.) When management did not concede to unions the right to exist, a deadly disagreement was marked (occasional volcanic outbreaks of violence apart) by a deadly silence. So long as Judge Gary did not recognize the existence of unions he obviously did not trade insults with their leaders.

Involved here, in fact, is the not inconsiderable difference between the tactics of homicide and those of negotiation. When a man has decided to murder another, he does not play to the gallery. He is unlikely to be much concerned with public opinion. He does not find it necessary to seek relief for his feelings or from his frustrations in words. He goes out and dispatches his man quickly and as quietly as possible. This was the nature of labor relations prior to the thirties. It was quiet and even for the most part orderly, not because there was agreement but because there was a total absence of agreement. In the South, at present, we have fewer strikes and fewer charges and countercharges between employees and employers than in the rest of the country. The reason is not that there is better understanding but that there is less understanding. Among Western European coun-

tries, Spain has the fewest labor disputes, not because labor relations there are better than
elsewhere, but because they are nonexistent.

### III

The noise that now characterizes the practice of
labor relations is of two sorts. In part it is traditional—a formal ritual of denunciation, required
equally of labor leaders and management, and not
meant to be taken seriously. The NAM orator just
mentioned who called for a crusade against unions
under the euphemy of labor monopoly was, without much doubt, merely performing a rite. None
would have been more surprised than he had his
audience stormed out of the Waldorf-Astoria
shouting its determination to extirpate all offend-
ing unions, root and branch. In fact, the speaker
did not expect his audience to do anything.

The debate over the Taft-Hartley Act, and the
questions of its amendment and repeal, is especially influenced by tradition. When the Taft-
Hartley Act was enacted in 1947, it was easy to
regard it as an attack on the principle of union
coexistence. Employers before had accepted
unions, bided their time, and then struck back.
Presumably they were doing it again. And the
fears of the union leaders in this regard were
probably no more exaggerated than the hopes of
numerous of the act's supporters. This set the tone
of the controversy over the Taft-Hartley Act. So it

has continued. The Taft-Hartley Act has no doubt caused considerable discomfort to the unions and has had an important effect on organization in the South. But it certainly has not destroyed unions. Though it may have improved the employer's tactical position, it has contributed little to the strategic goals of those who hoped it might rid them of unions. Yet such is the influence of tradition that we have continued, at least until comparatively recent times, to debate the Taft-Hartley law as though the great question of union survival were involved. This question alone could justify the invective which the union leaders have poured upon it. And this alone could justify the religious emotion with which some of the act's most inconsequential features have been defended by its friends. It is hard to see, incidentally, why the friends of the Taft-Hartley law are so pleased by it. As noted, many had hoped it might rid them of the incubus of the union. It did not. Theirs is a far deeper cause for dissatisfaction and frustration than that of the union leaders. These defenders are the men who should feel cheated.

## IV

The other cause of the continuing noise in labor relations is the peculiar nature of the transaction that occurs between union and employer. It involves a trial of strength between the contending parties, and both the general framework of law surrounding collective bargaining and the state of public opinion can be important sources of strength or weakness to one party or the other. Because public attitudes are a factor in the strength of the contending parties, the issues in any collective bargaining contest must be kept prominently in the public domain. It is for this reason that, during the course of normal collective bargaining, charges and countercharges, threats and counterthreats are communicated to the public with meticulous care. The public, for its part, is responsive to any relief from the tedium of an excessively peaceful existence. It has come to look to collective bargaining for some of the belligerency of a prize fight or an election. Realizing this, the newspapers and the news commentators do their best not only to dramatize the conflict but also, by emphasizing the disastrous effects on the community, to give their audience an agreeable sense of personal involvement.

It need hardly be stressed that neither the aspect of mortal conflict nor the aura of community crisis which surrounds so much of the collective bargaining process is any real measure of the stress in labor relations. Both are often synthesized; their effect is primarily on those existentialist souls who are able to rise to the heights of alarm or moral indignation one day without realizing that they will have forgotten all about it the next. Any

American of more than twenty can recall numerous strikes—the stoppage of the railroads in 1946, the time when Truman tried to seize the steel mills, the moment when the New York newspapers were silenced. On each of these occasions the foundations of the republic were held to be crumbling —at least for a day or two. In his recent memoirs, Cyrus S. Ching, the country's pioneer labor mediator, offers a more rational view of the matter. "I don't think this country, as a whole, ever really suffered seriously as a result of a strike in the last fifty years."[7]

One indication of the partly synthetic character of the normal labor crisis is its inability to sustain conversation after the fact. Murder, rape, fire, flood, and other such legitimate catastrophes can be savored for many weeks. So to some extent can such exercises in organized or spontaneous belligerency as a prize fight, a World Series, or a local knife battle. But all discussion of a strike normally dies on the day a new contract is signed. The sound and fury which so commonly mark our collective bargaining tell nothing of the state of rapport in our labor relations. They show only that the process of collective bargaining is being conducted normally.

[7] Cyrus S. Ching, *Review and Reflection*. New York: Forbes, 1953, p. 103.

## V

For appraising the state of conflict and agreement in economic life the nature of the accommodation in the labor market is, perhaps, the most important datum of all. This is the oldest arena of conflict in capitalism. Here is the naked choice of whether the boss will be boss or not—whether he will be able to exercise authority over wages and working conditions and enjoy unimpaired powers of command, or whether he will share this authority. Economic life poses few more obscenely naked problems of prestige and of power and also of income. And it offers few more opportunities for righteous indignation. Rarely have employers been open to persuasion on the point that they maltreat their workers; it is not easy to show that a divided command will be as efficient as a unified one. No one should take so Christian a view of mankind as to suppose that such issues could ever be easily resolved.

They have not been easily resolved, and much modern social and political history could be written in terms of attempts at resolution. Germany and Italy, in their days of fascist aberration, sought a resolution by eliminating the union as an independent force. Unitary control of the labor market was reaffirmed in the hands of the employer. This must have looked to German and Italian employers like an exceedingly plausible and stable solution. In fact, it resulted only in a state of suppressed revolution. The communist countries have also established a unitary control of the labor market by the euthanasia of both employer and independent union and the substitution of the state as the total arbiter. As to the stability of this arrangement we have as yet no demonstration. We can properly speculate on its consistency with the freedom and dignity of the individual.

There remains only the implausible arrangement of the modern Western democracy. Therein the power in the labor market is shared by the principals. Marxian literature leaves us no hope that this pluralism will work. Employers will first destroy the unions and then be destroyed. The contemporary right-wing literature is no more reassuring. Unions are rapacious and will eat up capitalism unless they are first destroyed. And it is clear that a stable pluralist solution is not easily achieved. In the United States our journey to the present organization of the labor market severely taxed our capacity for sustaining law and order. No inconsiderable number of men lost their lives while the solution was being sought, and some still do. Yet it is apparent that, once achieved, a plural control of the labor market does provide a stable solution. That is our experience. It is confirmed by the experience of the United Kingdom, Scandinavia, the British Commonwealth countries, It may actually be the only stable solution for, clearly, such divided control working through collective bargaining does not repress any revolutionary impulses, and it may be the only arrangement of which this can be said.

In any case it can safely be concluded that the element of conflict in labor policy has been enormously reduced in the last twenty years. The magnitude of the present conflict is, indeed, not comparable with that of the old. What was an issue of life and death is now, in the main, one of bargaining tactics. The latter still uses the harsh and uncompromising language of another era. But we make a great mistake if we fail to see that, while the sound is the same, the fury is not.

# THREE

# The Controversy over Bargaining Power

THE struggle in the labor market, with the accompanying controversy, was the consequence of an original inequality in bargaining power and the efforts of the union to redress it. Such inequality is not peculiar to the labor market, nor are the consequences to which it gives rise. There is a similar problem wherever numerous, and for that reason individually powerless, persons do business with few, large, and for that reason relatively more powerful, firms.[1] This is the weakness of the individual worker; it also broadly characterizes the situation of the farmer. The individual farmer typically has no influence over the price at which he sells or buys. He lives in a world where, as the result of a stronger market position in other quarters, some power to influence prices is commonplace. This does not necessarily mean that the farmer is subject to overt maltreatment or exploi-

---

[1] J. K. Galbraith, *American Capitalism, The Concept of Countervailing Power*. Boston: Houghton Mifflin, 1952.

tation by his intrinsically more powerful customers or suppliers, although such exploitation cannot be excluded as a fact of history. The difference in market power does mean that the modern price economy, a cherished preconception to the contrary, treats different groups very differently. In particular, in times of declining demand the weak market position of the farmer manifests itself in a prompt drop in his prices. He is without power to prevent this happening. By contrast, most of those with whom he does business are in a position to exercise some influence on the prices at which they sell or at which they buy, or on both. The farmer's lack of market power in a world where a measure of power is commonplace means that the terms of trade will turn sharply against him when demand declines. His prices fall; the prices he pays fall far less rapidly. This is a feature of the farmer's position as this is written. It has been an invariable feature of all depressions, serious or incipient, for many years. It is not a course of events which the farmer has ever relished. On the contrary, this sense of special vulnerability and weakness, the counterpart of the absence of bargaining power, has long been a major underlying cause of agrarian agitation and discontent.

Viewing his weakness in bargaining power, the worker was never in doubt as to the appropriate solution. It was to form a union. The farmer's vision of his problem and its solution has never been so definite. He has sometimes sought to turn the terms of trade in his favor by monetary tinkering and inflation. He has sought at other times to reduce the power of those with whom he did business either by subjecting them to state regulation or subjecting them to the antitrust laws. Voluntary associations for enhancing bargaining strength— the cooperatives—have at times looked to be the solution. In the end, however, in the United States, as in virtually all other Western countries, the government has come to intervene in markets in order to influence them in the farmer's favor.

## II

As with collective bargaining and plural control of the labor market, this redress of the farmer's bargaining position has been a rich source of controversy. The nature and purpose of the government's intervention here have never been seen with any such clarity as the purposes of the union. The assumption that an unmanaged or "free" price system accords equal treatment to all meant that intervention on behalf of the farmer had a strong flavor of special privilege. Certainly it has seemed a far less logical answer to larger power across the market than the union. Finally, the argument over whether anything should be done to redress the farmer's weakness in the market has always been confused with the argument over what should be done; and this is still the case.

Nevertheless, it is possible to conclude that in

the case of agriculture, as in the case of labor, the great issue of principle has now been resolved. The agricultural counterpart of whether unions should exist is whether the government should intervene in farm markets. On the latter there is still a greater difference of commonly expressed opinion than there is on the subject of the legitimacy of the union. But the effective difference of opinion—effective in relation to political action—is little if any greater.

The change for agriculture has come roughly in the last twenty-five years. In the twenties, the principle of government intervention to support the bargaining position of the farmer was debated and flatly rejected. In vetoing the first McNary-Haugen Bill, the first frontal effort at large-scale intervention, President Coolidge took his stand firmly on grounds of principle. He was interdicting a policy, he suggested, which had "alike no justice and no end . . . an economic folly from which this country has every right to be spared." Into the thirties the Republican party took its stand in opposition to the idea of intervention as such.

· It seems probable that as late as the election of November 1952 many people believed they were voting for the abolition of supports to farm prices and controls on farm production. And in his first press conference after taking office, even Secretary of Agriculture Ezra Taft Benson suggested that price supports would henceforth be used only as insurance against "undue disaster." But, in the

year and a half since, the new administration has
been at pains to show—as, indeed, was General
Eisenhower as a candidate—that it fully accepts
the principle of giving support to the farmer's
markets. "For many reasons," President Eisenhower told the Congress in a message on agriculture early in 1954, "farm products are subject to
wider price fluctuations than are most other com-
modities. Moreover, the individual farmer or
rancher has less control over the prices he receives
than do producers in most other industries. Government price supports must, therefore, be provided in order to bring needed stability to farm
income and farm production."[2] Such language
allows no doubt as to the full acceptance of the
principle of intervention in these markets.

### III

In recent months there has been an active debate
on farm policy, but this must be taken as another
illustration—an admirable one, in fact—of the lack
of relationship between the energy of debate and
the importance of the issue. The administration
has proposed that farm prices, or more specifically
those of corn, cotton, wheat, rice, and peanuts,[3] be

[2] *Farm Message.* H. Doc. No. 292, 83rd United States Congress,
2nd Session. *Congressional Record,* January 11, 1954, p. 113.

[3] Tobacco, also a "basic" crop and receiving mandatory support, is unaffected by the new legislation.

supported in accordance with a so-called flexible system of price guarantees. Under this arrangement, the guaranteed price would decline as supplies on hand or in prospect increase. This is in contrast with arrangements, hitherto in effect, by which the prices of these products are guaranteed at predetermined levels regardless of supply.

The critical point, however, is not the rigidity of the guarantee but the fact that both arrangements do accept market intervention to support farm prices. What was once the great issue concerning the scope of government responsibility is no longer an issue at all. All that is now involved is a question of method. And it should be added that even the difference in method is minor. Since present stocks of the agricultural staples which receive support are generally large, the effect of a system of support prices which relates the level of support to supply would be to lower prices to levels indicated by large supply. To avoid this effect, present cotton and wheat stocks will be sterilized, i.e., it will be pretended that they do not exist. The effect of this and other compromises is to make prospective flexible prices about as favorable as the present rigid prices. Immediately at stake in the current row over farm policy are a negligible change in cotton prices, a matter of five or ten cents a bushel in the case of corn, and perhaps as much as twenty-five or thirty cents a bushel in the case of wheat. There is no indication that the reduced prices under the administration plan will have any appreciable effect on production and, accordingly, on the accumulation of surpluses or the need for controls. Thus, in these respects, there is no change in the policy hitherto followed. It may be added that all of the faults of the recent farm programs, which are formidable, are continued by the proposed new policy.

## IV

None of this, it is worth repeating, would be evident from the current debate over farm policy. From the latter it could only be assumed that great questions were at stake. This, to be sure, is partly because farm policy is, as subjects of controversy go, a fairly old one. Around any old topic, the atmosphere of controversy tends, in a measure, to become institutionalized. It is taken for granted by everyone that where labor is involved or where farmers are concerned there will always be a row. No one any longer looks further to see whether the row is important or not.

In addition, there is, as on numerous other subjects of controversy, a certain vested interest in dispute. This is partly intellectual. Issues like the St. Lawrence Waterway, until its approval in 1954 the Methuselah of economic arguments, have the standing of old friends in relation to the disputants involved. One can relax. On such a topic there is no new research to be done, there are no new facts to be learned. The alignment of allies and enemies and constituents is tolerably certain, so a man can know where he stands. It is hardly surprising that when such an issue comes along it is debated with enthusiasm. Unfamiliar issues— those involving, for example, atomic energy, which, unlike the St. Lawrence River, might conceivably liquidate both the disputants and those who elect them—have no similar capacity to stir up debate.

However, the vested interest in argument is by no means exclusively intellectual. It derives also from an intelligent appreciation of problems of dollars and cents. On such a subject as farm policy —by no means an extreme case—there are some hundreds of influential and articulate people whose livelihood depends on the existence of a difference of opinion. In recent times the income and way of life of those who have fought the battles for butter and for oleomargarine have undoubtedly compared favorably with those who produce the materials that go into these ancient antagonists. I would not suggest that the fiscal interest in a good quarrel causes any reputable citizen to go out and promote a fight. Such an interest is not the strongest possible inducement for joining battles. But the existence of vested interest in controversy may be one of the reasons why the latter has a life and a dynamic apart from the issues involved.

It is one of the reasons why, in economic argument, the vilification lingers on.

The peculiar viability of old arguments is, indeed, one of the great facts of history. Long after the question of Empire versus Papacy had ceased to divide the Ghibellines and the Guelphs—long, indeed, after they had forgotten what issue divided them—they continued to quarrel with only slightly abated ardor. For similar reasons, Irishmen continue to fight Cromwell and more recent Englishmen; old-fashioned colonialism seems a more viable enemy to numerous Asian intellectuals than the hegemony of the Soviets; the poll tax until recently was almost (though not quite) as important in the South as the price of cotton; and numerous American conservatives continue to campaign against Roosevelt.

## V

So far we have learned two lessons. First there is the simple one of fact. On two of the most important subjects of controversy in our time, labor and farm policy, the real issue has been resolved. A struggle, which once involved a great change in the power relationships in the American economy, has subsided into a skirmish over the terms of the ultimate accommodation. For the peace and well-being of the American economy and polity these are facts of importance. As has been truly said on other matters, a poor peace is preferable to any war.

But we also learn one more thing from this experience. In these areas of controversy the resolution of the issue brings no subsidence in the noise of battle. The latter has a life that is separate from the issue itself. Indeed, the guns may be at their loudest when they are firing blank ammunition.

# FOUR

# The General Economics of Argument

A TOLERABLE accommodation in the labor market is, without much doubt, the most important single requirement for tranquility in the modern community. Argument on some other economic questions can be severe and exceptionally long-winded, but on no other matter does it have the same tendency to incite the use of truncheons, pistols, stones, brass knuckles, and similar supplements to purely verbal emphasis.

Such are the probable facts. However, it is widely assumed in the Western democracies that the most ardent debate will be over a much more cosmic issue, that it will be concerned with the ultimate shape and form of the economic and political society the community is to have. Will it be capitalist or socialist or communist? What will be the character of related political institutions?

It must be said that while it is widely *assumed* that these are urgent issues, they are not much debated in this form in the United States. There are, for the time being at least, almost no spokesmen for an alternative to capitalism. All of the important economic groups in the United States—businessmen, workers, farmers, intellectuals, and professional and white-collar groups—identify themselves vigorously with orthodox capitalism. So it is with the political parties. There is currently no sizeable political group which seeks the discontinuance of private ownership and management of the greater part of all productive resources, or which opposes the private receipt and enjoyment of most of the fruits of production. Some such platform is inevitable for any group which seeks by whatever means a socialist or communist alternative to the present economy.

The low estate to which socialism has fallen in the United States is indeed one of the more remarkable events of our time. This is no doubt partly the result of our much-discussed pressures for conformity. In no other modern country has capitalism had such energetic and articulate defenders, and they have frequently been a trifle self-righteous and uncharitable to those who disagreed. Still it is hard to suppose that such pressures have much increased in recent times. Socialists were under heavy pressure thirty-five years ago when, nonetheless, Eugene V. Debs polled a million votes for the Presidency, and with the added handicap of being in the Atlanta Penitentiary. The fact that few people feel terribly discontented with their lot is a plausible explanation of the highly nonrevolutionary mood of the moment.

Debate on capitalism and socialism is not, to be sure, wholly absent. There is the continuing debate over what may be termed guileless and clandestine socialism. It has long been popular doctrine that although there are but few forthright socialists in the United States, there are many who would achieve the same result by advocating individual measures which in the aggregate amount to socialism. Some, the guileless, are innocent of any design. Others, the clandestine socialists, know exactly what they are about but do not breathe a word concerning their motives. To quote a typical alarmed believer in the clandestine concept: "... there is [in the United States] steering, and crafty steering, toward the national socialist state by those who know exactly what they want and how to get it. If they succeed, there will be the terrors of confiscation and concentration camps."[1] What is called national socialism here, it may be observed, carries no connotation of Nazism; the author, following a common practice, is fortifying the word socialism to make it more adequately alarming. As the danger of socialism has retreated in the United States, there has been a tendency for that term to take on a connotation of mild and harmless political eccentricity. It requires buttressing.

The debate over the individual measures which are presumed to comprise guileless socialism will

[1] Harley L. Lutz, *A Platform for the American Way*. New York: Appleton-Century-Crofts, 1952, p. vii.

be examined presently. It is evident that clandestine socialism cannot involve any real argument, for if its clandestine exponents were to defend it, they would lose their clandestine standing. However, it is hard to suppose that the number of people who combine the position, wisdom, and restraint to work secretly, and (unlike the communists) apparently independently, to achieve large socialist ends can be very large. Our political and social traditions what they are, it is hard to see how the clandestine socialists could make much progress without holding an occasional convention.

It should also be noted that even the conservative fears of guileless and clandestine socialism seems to have been retreating in recent times. Speaking before the National Association of Manufacturers in the autumn of 1953, Mr. Sinclair Weeks, the Secretary of Commerce, suggested that of late "A climate favorable to business has *most definitely* [italics added] been substituted for the socialism of recent years."[2] Nothing so sanguine had been suggested at an NAM meeting for many days. (Mr. Weeks' view of socialism as something that comes and goes like bad weather is not un-

[2] "Business in a Growing America." Address by The Honorable Sinclair Weeks, at the 58th Session of the Annual Congress of Industry, National Association of Manufacturers, New York City, December 2, 1953. New York: National Association of Manufacturers, 1953.

common, and his optimism was endorsed a few weeks later by no less a figure than the President of the United States Steel Corporation. "The United States has had a close call," he said. "It was taken on a long detour toward Socialism . . . we have turned and now face toward private capitalism. . . ."[3])

In sum, it is evident that disagreement concerning the broad outlines of the American economy is within a larger framework which accepts and, indeed, takes for granted the general idea of a capitalist society. Thus, once again our argument does not extend to the fundamental question of principle. Unlike contemporary Italy, France, and, although in decidedly more ambiguous form, the United Kingdom, the basic structure of the economy is not at issue. Frenchmen and Italians might observe with some justice that we make a much more obscene racket in the course of living with our nearly nonexistent communists than they do in surviving with their millions. If we are to keep matters decently in perspective, we must have this general acceptance of a capitalist society well in mind as we proceed to examine the arguments over how that society should be shaped or governed. For again, the really fundamental question is not at issue.

3 Speech by Clifford F. Hood, at the Traffic and Transportation Club, Birmingham, Alabama, February 4, 1954. Quoted in the *U. S. Steel Quarterly*, February 1954.

## II

There are two questions concerning the broad structure and government of our economy which have been subjects of acute controversy in the last twenty-five years. The first and in some respects the least understood of these issues concerns the extent to which capitalism can be counted upon to turn in a reliable performance if left to itself. To what extent do economic stability and growth depend on proper guidance of the economy by the federal government? The second controversy is over the more familiar problem of the proper scope of government activities, and particularly those activities which have come to be identified with what is called the Welfare State.

The first of these disagreements seems rather straightforward. In one view the American economy in peacetime works automatically. In the other view, it is held to require careful and at times comprehensive guidance by the government. The common test of performance here is the capacity of the economy to maintain something close to full employment. In the first view, the economy if left to itself may not offer employment to all willing workers at all times and under all peacetime circumstances. But it will come close. And it will provide more employment with less ancillary damage to the freedom, moral stamina, or long-run economic well-being of the population than if the government tries to do something about it. There is a basic presumption in this view that the long-run consequences of any government action are intrinsically bad.

In the second view there is no reason to assume automatic good performance from the American economy. Left to itself, the economy will, on frequent occasions, leave willing men without work, and the production of goods that is lost during these periods of depression (or even stagnation) is lost forever. The unmanaged economy may also commit itself to bouts of serious and possibly prolonged inflation—periods when prices rise senselessly and with serious hardship to those in the community whose incomes or assets do not rise in keeping with the price advance. The counterpart of this view is the conviction that the government can do something about it. Strong and effective guidance of the economy by the government will insure good performance.

Obviously this is a formidable difference of opinion. However, the real sources of the dispute over this issue lie yet deeper. They are identified with the considerable consequences for social attitude and action which come from accepting the one view of the economy or the other. Specifically, if the economy is viewed as essentially automatic in its behavior, government in the modern state can be relatively simple and inconsequential. Unless the economy is viewed as automatic, it is impossible to envisage a government that is simple and uncomplicated.

The point is readily established. A government which assumes no responsibility for the guidance or direction of the economy, is confined in its activities to the execution of those tasks which the people or their representatives believe to be of common benefit and worth their cost in taxes. These activities may be numerous or few depending on the opulence of the community and its preference for collectively, as compared with individually, enjoyed goods and services. The problem of what the government will do and spend, though perhaps never an easy one, is, under these circumstances, a wholly comprehensible one. And the tests of good public housekeeping are the same as of good private housekeeping. Income should cover outgo; only emergency or peculiar urgency of need justifies incurring any debt.

When the assumption of automatic good performance in the economy is denied, and when the need for government guidance of the economy is conceded, these comfortable and comprehensible standards of what government should be like no longer hold. Government is no longer simple, nor is it likely that it can be very small. Since the stability and performance of the economy are now a *sine qua non*, government spending must be assessed not by the services it renders, but by the contribution it makes to stability.

Thus public works, housing, power development, reclamation, are no longer, by the infinitely subjective mensuration of politics, justified by the desire of the people for these things and their willingness to pay for them or to have their well-to-do neighbors do so. The critical question is now the effect of these activities on production and employment and prices in the economy at large. Now there is the possibility that the needs of the country for employment may be more nearly decisive than its needs for a new dam. Or highly desirable enterprises may have to be postponed in order to prevent excessive investment and consequent inflation in the country at large.

Equally intricate judgments must be brought to bear on taxation. Taxes are no longer, simply, the collective discomfort by which needed services are paid for. The goal of tax policy is no longer to see that taxes are paid by those who can best afford them or benefit most from the services. Taxes must now be considered in relation to consumer spending and business investment, of which they are the principal device for encouragement or restraint.

The old tests of fiscal sanity and morality also no longer hold. When depression threatens, income should not cover outgo and a deficit is a mark of fiscal wisdom and virtue. At other times, needed public functions and services must be foregone, unneeded taxes must be levied, and a redundant surplus must be accumulated in order to check inflation. While there is nothing, by the old standards, that is seemingly so iniquitous as a planned deficit, there is nothing more paradoxical than that parsimony should be most needed amidst the greatest opulence.

These are only a few of the complexities which are introduced when the notion of automaticity is abandoned. At deeper levels of intricacy the size of the budget, even though it is always balanced, has a bearing on the way the economy functions. Because of such complexities, the citizen finds the government invaded by an economic priesthood which is privy to the mysteries. In the physical sciences we take for granted that the intricacies of the phenomena involved will, at any early stage, pass beyond the comprehension of the ordinary man. But in the region of social phenomena we still insist on simplicity. Problems of economics and government were meant to yield to straightforward, plain common sense, and if they don't they should. (The individual who suggests that things are really more complicated is only revealing his own predisposition to involuted, oversophisticated, ostentatious, and erroneous complexity.) Nothing has caused the businessman and the politician to cling more ardently to the assumption of automaticity than the complexity of the judgments which follow its rejection.

## III

But more than simple and comprehensible government is at stake in the issue of automaticity as against the guided economy. A whole new standard of public ethics is also involved. Policies which once were advanced on humanitarian and egalitarian grounds become functional. It is readily shown that they make the economy work better. Things that once were honest special privilege become damaging to the public.

Thus one of our cherished activities in the United States is that of entering vigorous public petition on behalf of purely private interest. On taxation, the tariff, preferential regulation, the acquisition, use, or exploitation of public resources, on government contracts, and a hundred other matters, there is a constant, highly organized, and frequently ingenious effort to win special favors. Two rules govern this effort: There must be no outright bribery. It must be contended, however spuriously, that a public interest is being served. Self-interest, in other words, must wear a decent cloak. The manufacturer who seeks a higher tariff must do so in the name of his employees and the good American community in which they live. The taxpayer who seeks lower taxes must explain how they will be reinvested to make more jobs, and how the added incentive will stimulate his energies. The theft of public

resources must be shown to represent an enlight-
ened stand against collectivism and socialism and
on behalf of individualism and free enterprise.

If the economy is automatic in its operation,
then, obviously, it cannot be damaged by any
particular claim on behalf of private interest. It
works anyway. Accordingly, the resistance to special favors must be on purely moral grounds.
Someone must be prevented from getting something he does not deserve. This must normally be
done by someone who is enjoying favors or a job
he did not deserve.

When automatic performance by the economy
is not assumed, however, the standards of judg-
ment on all such matters are much more rigorous.
Special privilege stands condemned if it can be
shown to be a threat to economic stability. For the
latter is a serious matter. The responsibility for,
say, contributing to a serious depression is not one
that can be lightly assumed.

The inconvenience of such a standard was ad-
mirably illustrated during the 1954 debate on
tax policy. The Republican victory of November 1952 signified to many Americans the begin-
ning of the end of a long period in which tax
burdens had tended to become higher and increas-
ingly progressive, i.e., to rest with proportionately
greater weight on those with higher incomes than
with low. Some who savored this prospect became almost lyrical. "A New Federal Tax Policy:

The Words quicken the pulse and excite the imagination. They conjure up visions of fairness and
equity . . . of reviving incentives . . . of new hori-
zons . . . of more and better,"[4] a prominent American businessman told an audience in New York
the next autumn. His enthusiasm centered especially on reduction in the surtax brackets of the
personal income tax.

To justify such tax reduction by the ancient
American canon that a man is entitled to what he
can get away with would not have been difficult.
In the election the sympathies of the well-to-do
were generally with the Republicans. The Republicans won. This, surely, had established the moral
basis for some tax relief for the well-to-do. But
this was possible only if automaticity could be
assumed. Otherwise the action would have to be
examined for its effect on economic performance.
In the early winter of 1954, employment, production, income, and purchasing were declining at a
moderate rate. This was a reminder that tax
actions must be measured for their economic effect.

Such examination was far from favorable to the
hopes for higher-bracket tax relief. In drawing up
a formula for improving economic performance

[4] "Management's Role in Shaping a New Federal Tax Policy."
Address by Fred Maytag, Chairman, Taxation Committee, Na-
tional Association of Manufacturers, at the 58th Session of the
Annual Congress of Industry, National Association of Manu-
facturers, New York City, December 3, 1953. New York: National
Association of Manufacturers, 1953.

in time of threatening depression, the arguments are much, much stronger on the side of cutting taxes at the bottom of the income bracket than at the top. The spending of a man with two thousand dollars in income is likely to respond more promptly and more certainly to tax relief than that of a man with an income of two hundred thousand. For the same or similar reasons, an increase in sales taxes or a reduction in corporation taxes is difficult to defend.[5] In the twenties, Secretary Mellon could give a reduction in taxes to his fellow Republicans as a matter of course. Any justification in terms of better performance by the economy was at most an afterthought. In the fifties, however, Secretary Humphrey had no such good fortune. His tax concessions have had to run the gamut of a searching consideration of their effect on economic behavior, and, as this is written, it is still far from certain that they will find permanent acceptance.

[5] It is argued by conservatives, who would not assert the automaticity of the economy, that the incentive effects of corporate or higher-bracket tax reduction on individual effort and on investment are favorable to economic performance. (*Hearings before the Joint Committee on the Economic Report*, Congress of the United States, 83rd Congress, 2nd Session, February 2, 1954. Washington: U. S. Government Printing Office, 1954, pp. 51-55.) However, arguments based on the incentive effects of tax reduction suffer from three grave disabilities, to wit: they are subjective; they have been used excessively and indiscriminately in the past to justify any desired tax relief; and, in so far as individual effort is concerned, they carry the disagreeable implication that the individual making the plea for a better incentive for himself is presently not doing his best.

Further consequences follow from the rejection of the notion of automatic good performance by the economy. Profits are now appraised not by the standards of whether they are earned, deserved, or subject to the nine-point rule of possession, but by the evidence of whether they are favorable for economic performance. Trade union leaders on occasion find it possible to reinforce their claims with the assertion that more pay would increase consumer spending and add to economic stability. Even so small a matter as a tariff increase or a boost in steel prices may develop these larger economic implications. Conflicting with the latitude anciently allowed for returns to power, privileged interests, amiable graft, or outright larceny, the abandonment of automaticity requires nearly everyone to be socially responsible in some respect at some time. No business decision is any longer quite private. Economic depression has been an unhappy experience with us. No one can lightly risk the charge that he is contributing to such a disaster.

## IV

Here, then, is the issue. One group of controversialists has sensed the dangers of depression (and, though with infinitely less alarm, also of inflation) if the economy is left to itself. This group has gone on to the conclusion that the government must act to insure good economic performance. Its adherents uniformly have argued that the intervention involved is by far the lesser evil and poses a far smaller threat to the survival of capitalism than the alternative instability. The government intervention required, they also hold, is not too uncomfortable—it is "the kind of planning which interferes a minimum with the underpinnings of capitalism (for example, consumers' sovereignty, the quest for profits, freedom to invest and work without central dictation)." In the main it consists of manipulation of the interest rate and of the tax and expenditure policies of the federal government. None of this implies any overt intervention in the decisions of the individual businessman. He is guided to decisions that are in keeping with good performance by the economy by indirect pressures that are indistinguishable, in general, from those of the free market.

In opposition to this sanguine view are those who have seen, or at least sensed, the dangers of abandoning the notion of automaticity which is implicit in all the above. They have seen that the notion of a guided economy is a Pandora's box filled with all sorts of political discomforts and social disciplines. They have not, accordingly, welcomed the ideas of those who have sought remedies for the instability of capitalism and in so doing have rejected the notion of automaticity. This is the chief reason for the suspicion which has come to surround the name of John Maynard Keynes in

modern times. Though he was a strenuous advocate of the measures by which full employment
might be achieved—and by which presumably the
reputation of capitalism for performance might
be saved—he also led the attack on the idea that
the modern capitalist economy found its equilib-
rium at full employment. To many conservatives
this made him as inimical a figure as Marx. There
have, in fact, been any number of proposals for a
witch hunt, with Keynesians rather than communists as the quarry. Among the evil aspects of Yale,
according to one of its undergraduates who, in
making the charges, climbed to brief notoriety a
year or so back, was its tendency to be "agnostic
as to religion, [and] 'interventionist' and Keynesian as to economics."[6] While the author was, on
the whole, neutral as between the evils of Godless-
ness and Keynes, others have been more disturbed
about the latter. The President of the United
States Steel Corporation has more recently com-
plained that businessmen are much better up on
the Bible than on the "perverted" doctrines of
Marx and Keynes.[7]

There is theoretically a third position that rejects
government guidance to prevent depression, and

6 William Buckley, Jr., *God and Man at Yale*. Chicago:
Regnery, 1951. The quotation is from the introduction by John
Chamberlin.

7 "Our Period of Decision," Speech by Clifford F. Hood, at
the Tenth Annual Lenten Corporate Communion Service of the
Episcopal Diocese of Pittsburgh, Pittsburgh, Pennsylvania,
March 27, 1954. New York: U. S. Steel Corporation, 1954.

also the notion of automaticity. This position would admit both of the possibility and of the need for an occasional depression. Then, without asserting the automatic character of economic performance, it would still be possible to argue against the need for government intervention. The latter, of course, is the objectionable corollary to the attack on automaticity.

As a purely intellectual proposition, an excellent case can be made for an occasional sharp (but preferably very short) depression. Through unemployment insurance, workers can be given a substantial measure of protection from a misfortune that is not of their making. At the same time, such a slump serves to remind the businessman that inefficiency and incompetence can be mortal. There is no such reminder from periods of prosperity. A depression returns to the labor force a variety of individuals who have escaped into industrial sinecures and "make-work" and who can no longer be afforded. It is also an admirable device for discouraging absentee administration of business enterprises from a seat in Florida, and it registers an apt penalty on the imprudent creditor and the improvident borrower. It is at least conceivable that depression in the short-run may lead to greater efficiency and productivity, a more rapid rate of economic growth, and greater prosperity in the slightly longer run.

However, the case for depression is one that very few Americans care to make, at least in public.

For a person of liberal sympathies to do so is unthinkable; nothing in our society would so certainly mark him as a surreptitious reactionary. But a conservative must be equally circumspect. He may speak cautiously of the virtues of a corrective recession. During the early months of 1954 a Princeton, New Jersey, banker even suggested that the economy required occasional moments of relaxation. "No machine can perform at top speed forever. There must be time for rest, overhaul, and adjustment if good performance is to be maintained."[8] For a prominent corporate executive, however, to advocate a depression either for its own sake or in preference to the government measures that might prevent it would be an impermissible heresy in our society. It would invite a censure almost as severe as that which would descend on the intellectual who argued the heroic values of a bloody revolution.[9] The argument that the econ-

---

[8] *New York Times*, May 6, 1954.

[9] Even in the intellectual environs of the NAM, the inevitability, not of depression but of any business fluctuations, is advanced with great circumspection. Thus a group of philosophers retained by the association a few years ago to identify the principles of free enterprise summarized their case for occasional depression in these notably cautious words: "With arbitrary authority and an obedient public, a government might provide full and steady employment while its power lasted; but some fluctuations must attend an economy in which the people have free choice." National Association of Manufacturers, Economic Principles Commission, *The American Individual Enterprise System, Its Nature, Evolution, and Future*. New York: McGraw-Hill, 1946.

omy does work all right if left to itself—that it is automatic—is therefore the only resort of those who cannot accept the consequences (including government intervention) which follow from the abandonment of the assumption of automaticity. We have here all the requisites of an argument, and, indeed, the argument has been sharp in our time. However, it is also an argument which has had its best days; in fact, it is far on the way to resolution. I now turn to the decay of the argument over automaticity.

# FIVE

## The Rejection of Automaticity

A MOMENT'S thought will suggest that those who have undertaken to argue the case for automatic good performance by the economy have a difficult case. Against them stands the great burden of practical experience. There are certain things palpably contrary to fact of which people can be persuaded. But this is possible, as a practical matter, only if they have no personal experience to the contrary.

The experience of overwhelming importance in relation to the assumption of automaticity was the Great Depression. Most Americans have experienced some other misbehavior of the economy, such as the rather drastic inflation following World War II and the mild slumps of 1949 and of (so far) 1953-54, but without doubt the catastrophic collapse and the dreary stagnation of the thirties were much more important. Everyone who argues for automaticity must face the question: What do you say about the depression?

To be sure, attempts have been made to recon-

cile the assumption of automaticity with the experience of depression. They have not been successful or even especially inspired. It has been
suggested that the depression was a unique occur-
rence, the result of a speculative orgy which was
itself the product of miguided government credit
policies during the twenties.[1] And it has been
argued that a normal recovery was frustrated by
the shock to confidence which resulted from the
election of the Democrats in 1932.[2] Neither of
these explanations has been wholly successful with
the American people. There is a further and in
some ways a more plausible contention that the
American economy prior to 1930 was one of peculiar weaknesses—the banking system was weak,
corporate structure had been subject to fiscal gerry-

[1] In the view of the NAM authors, for example, "Misdirected
governmental action contributed extensively to the conditions
leading to the 1929 debacle just as it did to the depression of
the nineties, of the seventies, etc." (National Association of
Manufacturers, Economic Principles Commission, *The American Individual Enterprise System, Its Nature, Evolution, and
Future.* New York: McGraw-Hill, 1946, p. 858.) In *A Study of
Depressions,* published in 1938, the association had previously
pointed out that "Recovery in the United States [was] less steady
than that of any other major industrial country." The reason
was that "the cumulative effect of government policies under-
mined confidence in the American economy and restricted the
1932-37 recovery."

[2] This thesis is argued with some certainty, although perhaps
not with equivalent plausibility, by Mr. Herbert Hoover in his
memoirs. (*The Memoirs of Herbert Hoover.* New York: Macmillan, 1951.)

mander, workers lacked minimum provision for social security, income and wealth were badly distributed—and that these and other shortcomings were corrected once and for all by the reforms of New and Fair Deals. Unhappily, such an argument gives an impossibly large endorsement to the therapeutic qualities of the two Deals. Those who argue most strongly for automatic good performances are, normally, those who are least inclined to give such credit. However, this argument, effectively summarized in the assertion that "the American economy is very different from what it was in 1929," is regularly offered.

While the defense of the assumption of automaticity foundered on the hard rock of practical experience, the opposing view acquired steady reinforcement. Two events might be singled out. There was, of course, the publication of Keynes' *General Theory of Employment, Interest, and Money* in 1936 and its immediate widespread influence on professional economic thought. There was also the formation in August 1942 of the Committee for Economic Development. The primary motivation of CED was the fear of what another depression might do to the reputation of American capitalism. At least initially, many of the business members of the organization hoped that by encouraging individual firms to plan for enlarged investment after the war it might be possible to forestall government planning. This looked like a plausible formula for escaping the seemingly untenable assumption of automaticity without adopting the unpalatable corollary of government responsibility. However, CED soon came to accept a conservative measure of government intervention as a requisite for good performance. And the rejection of automaticity by CED was explicit.[3] The defection of the CED businessmen was a serious blow to all who argued for the automatic economy. The fact that this was a business organization was especially damaging. In our tradition of economic debate, a proposition can often be more economically destroyed by association than by evidence. To assail a proposition as un-American, alien, wild-eyed, woolly, impractical, or pro-Communist is often effective and invariably more saving of time and energy than the somewhat obsolescent technique of dealing with an issue on its merits.

[3] A staff study of the CED published in 1946 which, though not an official expression of the organization's attitudes, can be taken as a fair indication of its position began as follows:

"As we take up the economic tasks of peace, two shadows fall over our shoulders:

"The shadow of 1919 and 1920: Prices zooming, up 25 per cent in a year. . . .

"The shadow of 1939—the end of two decades of 'peace.' After ten years of depression 9 millions were still unemployed. . . ." *Jobs and Markets*. New York: McGraw-Hill, 1946, p. 1.)

This strategy of attack has its counterpart in ideological defenses; indeed, it now involves something akin to a whole science of intellectual field fortifications. The underlying principle of this defense consists, again, of avoiding direct battle on issues and of finding and taking cover behind some individual or institution which is peculiarly invulnerable to the particular attack. Thus an individual who is attacked for a pro-Communist idea must promptly show that the same idea, or preferably a more extreme one, has been advanced by some member of the Catholic hierarchy or, at the least, a prominent Catholic layman. (Alternatively, it is useful to show that the same idea has been condemned in the *Daily Worker* or by *Pravda*.) The charge that an idea is radical, impractical, or long-haired is met by showing that a prominent businessman has favored it. Businessmen—successful ones at least—are, by definition, never radical, impractical, or long-haired.[4] It is obvious, in this context, that the rejection of the doctrine of automaticity by a group of influential businessmen was critical. The position of the CED was henceforth an important factor in the argument over automaticity and government intervention.

[4] There is an additional tactic in this strategy of defense which, for the sake of completeness, should be mentioned. That is to assert that Winston Churchill once sponsored the particular idea. If one is challenged, a sufficiently careful investigation will show that he did.

## II

The argument over automaticity versus government intervention in the economy is hardly a new one. And for at least a decade prior to the autumn of 1952 the issues in the debate and the alignment of the participants had been largely constant. The professional economists, their liberal business allies, and, with a good deal less explicit formulation of the problem, the unions rejected the notion of automatic performance. This view was broadly reflected in the platform and attitudes of the dominant New Deal-Fair Deal wing of the Democratic party. Asserting that things would be all right (and also much better) if left alone were the older business organizations, most people of conservative disposition, and the vocal conservative wing of the Republican party.

In this situation the victory of the Republicans in November of 1952 was crucial for the argument over automaticity. Until then it was possible for many to suggest and some to suppose that the notion of economic management was an evil invention of the Democratic party or that it was a mask for the power aspirations of political meddlers. And it could even be suggested that inflation or depression might be deliberately synthesized or exaggerated in order to give political functionaries an opportunity. "In past [Democratic] years whenever or wherever any question—even of minor consequence—arose, the government would label it a crisis. Undigested legislation would be rushed and rammed through the Congress. A new sprawling bureaucracy would be set up."[5] Assertion of this sort is not, to be sure, coordinate with belief. It is one of our well established conventions that the orator who wishes to make a point need not confine himself to the truth. His audience appreciates and applauds an impressive point which is impressive because it reflects what the listeners would like to believe even though they do not. Still, the doctrine of the synthesized crisis was a useful part of the intellectual support for the idea of automaticity.

Whatever charges might be leveled against a Republican administration, it was impossible to suggest that it sought to manage the economy as a matter of bureaucratic aspiration or that it would invent or exaggerate economic crises in order to extend its own power. At the same time, the Eisenhower administration has rejected the doctrine of automaticity and proclaimed the need for government guidance of the economy in language that is as unequivocal as that of its predecessors. "Government must use its vast power to help maintain

[5] "Business in a Growing America." Address by The Honorable Sinclair Weeks, at the 58th Session of the Annual Congress of Industry, National Association of Manufacturers, New York City, December 2, 1953. New York: National Association of Manufacturers, 1953.

employment and purchasing power as well as to
maintain reasonably stable prices," President Eisenhower told the Congress in his 1954 message accompanying the Economic Report.[6] He went on to
say that this "is not a start-and-stop responsibility,
but a continuous one," and he discussed at some
length the weapons—credit, controls, debt management, "flexibility in the administration of the
budget," agricultural price supports, tax policy, and
public works expenditures—which the government
has at its disposal for maintaining stability. He concluded, "We shall not hesitate to use any or all of
these weapons as the situation may require."[7] This
position leaves no room for doubt. And insofar as
the feelings of the more extreme opposition are
concerned, it would appear to be what Mr. John
T. Flynn once described as "hooded socialism"—
the tactic of using the danger of depression to
espouse an increase in government responsibilities
for its own sake and under the guise of saving
capitalism.[8] As a *New York Times* writer recently

[6] *Economic Report of the President,* transmitted to the Congress of the United States, January 28, 1954. 83rd Congress, 2nd
Session. Washington: U. S. Government Printing Office, 1954,
p. iv.

[7] Economic Report of The President, January 28, 1954.

[8] John T. Flynn, "The Road Ahead." Reprint of condensation
appearing *Reader's Digest,* February 1950, p. 10. As recently as
last March, Mr. Leonard W. Hall, Republican National Chairman, warned of the "Economic Fifth Column" which used a
world-wide depression of the thirties as a cover-up for its schem-
ing "and which is now seeking to raise the scarecrow of depression again." *New York Times,* March 5, 1954.

observed, "Having survived seventeen years of imaginative invective [the notion that the government must give all necessary support to the private economy] now crops up as a basic dogma of the Eisenhower Administration."[9]

## III

We may conclude, then, that there is now effective political agreement between the two major parties on rejecting the notion of economic automaticity and in accepting the need for government guidance to the economy. This agreement on principle does not imply agreement on method or detail. Nor has either party entirely eliminated all the ambiguities and the uncertainties from its position.

The first hope, naturally, of those who reluctantly accept the concept of government intervention is that the intervention will be slight and painless. This hope is father, or at least the stepparent, of the belief that stabilization can be accomplished by what economists have come to call monetary measures. By using its undoubted power to increase and decrease the supply of money— more specifically the supply of credit which banks and other lending agencies can make available to their customers—the government, it is held, can

9 Burton Crane, "The Business Bookshelf." *New York Times,* March 29, 1954.

regulate the level of economic activity. In poor times, relaxed credit and lower interest rates will encourage people to borrow, invest, and spend; when inflation threatens, tight money will force restraint and contraction. Such regulation is decent and decorous; the regulators are quiet, somber members of the infinitesimal elite which is privy to the recondite mysteries of money. They work from around a table. Their decisions are reached, not after raucous controversy, but after quiet discussion. It is regulation which involves no acts, orders, or regulations. Obviously, if the government must intervene in the economy, this is by far the most satisfactory way to do it.

Among professional economists there are few defenders of automaticity left. But the erstwhile defenders of this redoubt, or their spiritual descendants, have in recent years taken up their next position in defense of monetary policy as the principal or even the only necessary form of government intervention. This position has naturally been challenged by those who feel that much more comprehensive intervention is required. Some of the latter have gone on to argue that monetary measures are of little real consequence. Among economists the old argument over automaticity versus intervention has thus become one over whether the intervention can be confined to, or at least be dominated by, measures of a comparatively painless sort. In the inflation years following

World War II and during the Korean war the advocates of monetary controls have been especially vehement in arguing that inflation could have been checked by a rigorous use of these measures. Obviously these measures would have been much more agreeable than the additional instruments of management—heavy taxation and controls on prices and wages—which others considered necessary.[10]

This argument over methods of providing economic guidance has its counterpart in the political world. In general, New Deal and Fair Deal policy minimized the significance of monetary policy and made comparatively little use of it as an active instrument of control. The Republican party came to Washington in 1953 with a much larger commitment to monetary management. Some of the belief that this instrument was both politically painless and foolproof, however, was badly shaken by the ill-timed tightening of credit and increase in interest rates in the spring of 1953 and the ensuing need for a prompt reversal of the policy.

The use of public spending for economic management involves special difficulties for a conservative administration. As noted, the ancient test of fiscal sanity, when automatic economic behavior was assumed, was the balanced budget. The gov-

[10] Many, although not quite all, of those who argued that inflation could have been controlled in these years by monetary policy would also have urged high taxes.

ernment discharged *its* obligation to the economy by balancing its expenditures with income. This test is still an applicable one for states, cities, and municipalities which—the critical point—do not and cannot assume any important responsibility for the level of economic activity in the area they embrace. Few lessons have ever been learned so well as that of the balanced budget. A liberal government had to be for a balanced budget to show its responsibility. A conservative government had to be for a balanced budget to show that it kept faith with conservative principles. Especially, the balanced budget was an article of faith with conservatives.

But here is the tragic rub. The notion of government guidance of the economy is totally in conflict with the idea of a constantly balanced budget. Thus, when employment and income in the economy decline, tax revenues will fall. To keep the budget balanced tax rates should then be increased or expenditures reduced, or both. Such steps are flatly inconsistent with the goals of economic management. To increase taxes at such a time is to cause private spending to fall still more, with a further depressing effect on income and employment. (The increase in taxes might even cut income enough to cause total tax revenues to fall.) Similarly, when employment and incomes are falling, the accepted policy calls not for a cut in public expenditures but for an increase. Some of these increases—for payments to the unemployed and to underwrite farm prices—will indeed be automatic. Some, as for housing, public works, and the like, should be deliberately planned. If a government is to have a stabilization policy, if it is to reject the concept of automaticity, these are the things it must do. In other words, it must be prepared to have a deficit. There is no way by which it can disguise this decision; the action to create a deficit is deliberate. The balanced budget, the ancient hallmark of fiscal rectitude, has to be deliberately and publicly rejected.

From the viewpoint of the politician, especially the conservative, it is hard to see how the fates could have been more inconsiderate. The balanced budget is the symbol of all that is sane, sound, and respectable. It is the accepted safeguard against the undoubted temptation to public prodigality; by its simple rule-of-thumb, millions have been able to tell whether politicians were governing conservatively or wastefully. But such a policy cannot be reconciled with one of combating depression. And politically, the latter policy is even more compelling. More than anything else, the uncertainty over whether it had the will to such a policy was what blighted the fortunes of the Republican party between 1930 and 1952.

The reconciliation of these two irreconcilables— the balanced budget and the antidepression policy

—has involved, without doubt, some of the greatest of modern feats of politico-economic legerdemain. During the New Deal years the unbalanced budget was submitted as a purely passing phenomenon (a temporary aberration and a lesser evil) and defended by the intention to have a balanced budget next year. Toward the end of the thirties it was held, although with no great self-confidence, that a planned deficit could be a wise instrument of policy. But a balanced budget was still promised.

The Truman administration, which had both deficits and surpluses, was sometimes disposed to describe the first as inevitable and to cite the surpluses, when they appeared, as proving the predisposition to sound finance. Yet, during the postwar years there was a growing tendency for this administration to take a consistent view of the budget problem and to assert the policy of seeking a balance and surplus when employment and incomes were high and accepting a deficit when the economy required stimulation.[11]

This problem of reconciliation has been much more serious for the Republican party. As a conservative party, its commitment to the symbolism of the balanced budget is considerably stronger than that of the Democrats. During the years when

11 Such a position was articulated with caution, although also with some clarity, in the *Economic Report of the President,* transmitted to the Congress of the United States, January 6, 1950. Washington: U. S. Government Printing Office, 1950. See especially pp. 8, 11.

the party was in opposition, senior Congressional leaders, men like Congressman John Taber, the ranking member of the Appropriations Committee, identified their opposition with the issue of the budget. Yet, notwithstanding, the new administration has had to face the compulsions of stabilization policy. Especially in the 1954-55 budget (introduced in 1953) the tax and expenditure policies which would have eliminated the deficit were deemed far too dangerous to be adopted.

In part the new administration has utilized the New Deal technique of promising a balanced budget in the future. It has also undertaken the more novel line of reconciliation by proclaiming itself in favor of both a strong antidepression policy *and* a balanced budget. Not long after taking office, Secretary of the Treasury Humphrey, speaking of fears of forthcoming depression before the Associated Press, told his audience that "Plans for increased expenditures of funds for civilian needs are already under way in many quarters [of the federal government] and many more will follow. . . ." At the same time he expressed the view that it was essential "to bring our Federal expenditures under control and at the earliest possible time balance them with income."[12] This was perhaps the sharpest enunciation of the dual policy of increased and reduced spending and of combin-

12 *New York Times,* April 21, 1953.

ing deficit financing with a balanced budget. Nevertheless, the 1954 Economic Report promised a strong antidepression policy and included a reference to "flexibility in the administration of the budget."[13] It was accompanied by a declaration that the administration had charted "a fiscal and economic policy [designed to] reduce the planned deficits and bring the budget into balance."

It would be unwise, however, to make too much of these vagaries. It is more important that the Republican party has undertaken to liquidate its commitment to the continually balanced budget and, therewith, to the concept of the automatic economy. The escape from this commitment was bound to be embarrassing. It is hardly surprising that it was covered by a certain amount of disingenuous double talk.

## IV

There is a final subject of argument concerning economic management which deserves a word. This concerns not the action the government should take in the interest of better economic performance but the timing of such action. As this is written, such an argument on timing is in process, and it is one that we should expect to recur.

Even though there is agreement on the principle of government intervention in the economy, there

13 *Economic Report of the President,* January 28, 1954, p. iv.

will always be doubt as to whether the situation of the moment justifies a particular action. It can always be suggested that things are not yet bad enough to justify the action, and there can always be hope that if the action is withheld, things nonetheless will improve by themselves. A conservative administration is likely to delay action and to exploit fully the hope that prosperity will come around the corner by itself. It will be accused by liberals of being callous and negative, especially as the latter are in opposition.

It was once supposed by economists that empirical knowledge might, in effect, narrow the scope for this argument by providing a better insight into what the future might hold. This is an idle hope; there is no chance, given the present character and constitution of capitalism, that the techniques of economic forecasting will ever provide a basis upon which government action can be predicated. To suppose that this is possible may, indeed, be to deny the uncertainties that are inherent in capitalism.

On the contrary, the forecasts of economic behavior are likely to continue to be, as they are now and have been in the past, the handmaiden of the particular policy the forecaster is urging. As this is written in the spring of 1954, some three and one-half million people are unemployed; national income and output have been in a moderate decline. The administration has stated its conviction that the unemployment is temporary and that the decline in production soon will be reversed. This is not based on knowledge of the future. Indeed a high administration official has had the refreshing honesty to say so: "we ought to start right out on this premise . . . there is [no] man and probably never has been, and I think probably never will be, who can see very far into the future. . . . If there were . . . and he had the courage of his convictions, it would not be long before he owned almost everything and we would all be working for him."[14] The administration's forecast of recovery rather than further depression was derived from and was subordinate to a decision not to increase public works expenditures, institute broad-scale tax reduction, or take other steps to check a depression. At this same time, Democrats and trade union leaders have been urging the government to take action. As a result, they have been forecasting that the depression will get worse or at least that it will get no better by itself. Again, the forecast is based not on knowledge of the future but on the policy with which it is consistent and which it serves.

We have here the explanation of the frequency, vigor, and even vehemence with which forecasts of the prospective behavior of the economy are

[14] Honorable George M. Humphrey, Secretary of the Treasury. *Hearings before the Joint Committee on the Economic Report*, Congress of the United States, 83rd Congress, 2nd Session, February 2, 1954. Washington: U. S. Government Printing Office, 1954. p. 54.

offered in our time. This is not because the fore-casters know what is going to happen. It is not certain that they expect the public to believe that they know. Rather the forecasts are an aspect of advocacy. A powerfully articulated forecast of the conditions that will require a particular policy is an accepted part of every brief in support of a particular action. Public officials, politicians, lob-byists, and the generality of citizens regularly fore-tell the future as part of their case for (or against) public action. The public, in accordance with a well-established convention, listens respectfully to these forecasts but does not believe them. A state-ment by a Secretary of the Treasury that business will shortly improve, or one by a union leader that it will get worse unless the government acts has no effect on the stock market. Partly because no one believes such forecasts, there is little or no criticism when, with time, they are shown to be wrong.

However, all this goes somewhat afield. The problem of timing of economic action against de-pression is almost completely subjective. Accord-ingly, we may expect that conservatives and liber-als, even though agreed on the policy, will continue to divide on the question of whether the time has come to act.

## V

Arguments over the methods and the timing of government economic management can be severe.

There is also a grave question, as yet unanswered, of whether the techniques of economic management now subject to discussion are sufficient to secure the stability and growth of capitalism in face of all possible crises. But, as in the case of unions and farmers, it is once again evident that a controversy that once involved a major strategic principle has now become a secondary conflict over tactics. Not only is there agreement, for the time at least, on the larger constitution of a capitalist society, but there is also effective agreement on the principle of a socially guided or managed capitalism.

It must be stressed, nonetheless, that what has just been called *effective* agreement—agreement between the great interest groups and more especially between the major political parties—does not imply total agreement among all persons. The notion of deficit financing to sustain income and employment, in whatever semantic disguise, is not accepted by Senator Harry Flood Byrd. It is emphatically rejected by the right wing of the Republican party. The basic assumption of automaticity is still accepted by a good many hundreds of thousands and perhaps millions of people. To many of them this assumption, and the iniquity of government intervention, is regarded as a matter of divine ordinance.

This dissent, which manifests itself also in relation to the present agreement on labor and farm policy and numerous aspects of the Welfare State, is of much significance. The fact that it exists in face of a substantial agreement to the contrary between the major political parties means that it is without effective party expression and without hope of having its position prevail. At the same time it has strong individual voices in the national legislature and throughout the community. The way in which the frustrations of this minority color current economic discussion will be considered at some length in the final chapter.

# SIX

# The Welfare State

THE last great subject of economic argument during the last two decades has been the Welfare State. The name itself is the product of that dispute. As I have previously observed, it is a recognized and intellectually parsimonious tactic of debate in our time to destroy ideas by giving them disagreeable names. The effort to find a label which adequately condemns the government which assumes a large responsibility for the economic well-being of its constituents has caused difficulty. The appellations "socialist" and "communist," though much used, sound extreme. Like the cry of "wolf," moreover, they have been overdone. So many past actions have provoked the warning of socialism that if socialism were a danger we would already have it.

In the thirties, social insurance—unemployment compensation in particular—was condemned by the term "dole." It was confidently suggested that "No self-respecting American would ever accept a dole." This term lost its sting when several million self-respecting Americans showed a distinct willingness to accept a dole. In the years immediately following World War II, an effort was made to popularize the term "statism" for the purpose of characterizing and condemning too ubiquitous government. But it seems probable that the term sounded both artificial and not very alarming to most Americans. With us the term "state" inevitably connotes a state government, and, though we commonly regard such government as inept and none too honest, we are incapable of supposing it to be sinister.

The last of the efforts to devise a suitably unpalatable name for the phenomenon being condemned brought us the appellation "Welfare State." This achieved almost immediate currency but, unfortunately for its progenitors, without the unfavorable connotation it was meant to have. This was made clear in 1949 in a special senatorial in the state of New York, when Mr. Herbert Lehman ran against the briefly incumbent senator, Mr. John Foster Dulles. Mr. Dulles campaigned strenuously in opposition to the Welfare State. Mr. Lehman was in favor. Mr. Lehman won decisively. The lesson was read by Governor Thomas E. Dewey, a man of few political illusions, a few weeks later at Princeton. He said, "It must have been a very clumsy Republican" who sought to make political capital out of the term "Welfare State" and added, "Anyone who thinks an attack on the fundamental idea of security and welfare is appealing to the people is living in the Middle Ages."[1]

[1] *New York Times*, February 10, 1950.

It is improbable, in fact, that Mr. Dulles was attacking all or most security and welfare measures. Asked expressly about unemployment insurance, workmen's compensation, public education, or public assistance, he would no doubt have expressed some sympathy for them. This is the first thing that must be observed about the debate over the Welfare State, namely, the extreme uncertainty over what is being debated and the virtual certainty that an individual who opposes the Welfare State in the abstract will be in favor of much of it in the concrete. In the life of every individual there are times when his capacity for self-help is very low. In infancy he is not a dependable provider of his own livelihood, or in adolescence of his own education. Equally, he cannot be certain that in old age his unaided efforts will bring much income; his unaided efforts may then be worthless. Under some modern conditions, diligence and even a good deal of imagination may not be sufficient to find a job. Ill health has a tendency to cut down an individual's ability to help himself at a time when he most needs help. Welfare measures —the raw material of the Welfare State—are presumably the organized supplements to the individual's capacity for self-help.

Some of these supplements are certain to look reasonable to almost everyone. Thus even the most obdurate opponents of the Welfare State in the abstract will always be for some parts of it in practice. Among economists and social philosophers, Professor Ludwig von Mises has acquired a certain reputation, by no means unmerited, for the vigor with which over the last half century he has opposed virtually all forms of state intervention in the economy and in the life of the individual. He has suggested that all government is "in the last resort the employment of armed men, of policemen, gendarmes, soldiers, prison guards, and hangmen," and has added that its "essential feature" is the "enforcement of its decrees by beating, killing, and imprisoning."[2] He opposes government regulation of narcotics, not because he favors their use but because he believes that regulation of the dope peddler is an opening wedge to regulation of other forms of free enterprises. Professor Mises is a rugged opponent of the Welfare State; yet even Professor Mises makes exceptions. He is modestly in favor of public education: ". . . public education can work very well if it is limited to reading, writing, and arithmetic. With bright children it is even possible to add elementary notions of geometry, the natural sciences, and the valid laws of the country."[3]

Like Professor Mises, other ardent opponents of the Welfare State must always be in favor of some

[2] *Human Action*. New Haven: Yale University Press, 1950, p. 715.

[3] von Mises, p. 872.

of it. Some who are opposed in general may even
be sympathetic to all of the individual measures
that comprise the Welfare State. Indeed, a tendency
to abstract the whole entirely from its parts is a
feature of this debate. The government is seen as
reducing the individual to a pulpy dependence by
a proliferation of safe-guards and services. But each
of these latter—unemployment compensation, old
age insurance, aid to dependent children and the
blind, workmen's compensation, provision for public education—is approved in itself. Speaking in
Boise, Idaho, during the 1952 election campaign,
General Eisenhower observed that things had now
reached the point where "The government does
everything but come in and wash the dishes for the
housewife." Later, to the delight of all, he was able
to produce a pamphlet of the United States Depart-
ment of Agriculture which showed that the government actually advised the housewife on how to
wash dishes. Although General Eisenhower was
firm in his condemnation of the paternalism of the
New and Fair Deals, the unfortunate pamphlet was
the only specific service which he attacked. Nearly
all of the remainder he promised to strengthen.
Since he took office, no important welfare services
have been withdrawn. Even the pamphlet on how
to wash dishes has enjoyed unprecedented popu-
larity and has gone through several more editions.

President Conant once said of Harvard that it was not coeducational in principle, only in practice.

In sum, the argument over the Welfare State is at its best only when the concept is divorced entirely from its substance. A case can be built up against the notion of a society in which the individual pillows his head on the lap of a too tender government, but it cannot easily be sustained against the individual caress. This need to keep the argument over the Welfare State on a high level of abstraction is, perhaps, its greatest source of weakness as the subject of a row. It is the first reason for thinking that, as in the case of unions and the issue of automaticity versus intervention, this subject of controversy too may have seen its best days.

## II

Although the Welfare State in general may not be a succesful subject of controversy, there is still an opportunity for argument over individual measures. These must, however, be measures which are not yet a matter of experience, for here we encounter another curious feature of the argument in this area. Debate is almost invariably confined to measures that have not yet been enacted. One of the most surprising features of social welfare legislation is its inability to sustain controversy once it has passed into law. At this writing, seven years after the passage of the Taft-Hartley Act, the latter is still a subject of controversy. The Wagner Act sustained a sharp controversy throughout the preceding decade. The persisting contentiousness of our farm laws has been noted. In other areas, such as immigration, internal security, and power policy, disagreement is more or less chronic and is little affected by passage or rejection of laws by the legislature. With the help of Senator Bricker the treaty power under the Constitution is still an issue after 175 years.

By contrast, the social welfare legislation now on the statute books is almost entirely noncontroversial. It became so promptly on enactment and despite the acute preceding row. This is not our own experience alone. Lloyd George's National Insurance proposals of 1911, the precursor of our social security legislation, provoked one of the most strenuous debates in British history. Some have even gone so far as to suggest that this was the only period in modern British history when the violence of political emotions was sufficient to threaten orderly constitutional process.[4] But no sooner had the measures become law than the controversy ceased. What was forecast to be Britain's final ruin quickly became the platform of all parties. The same experience was repeated, much less arduously, in 1946 with the enactment of the Beveridge proposals, particularly the National

[4] Tax increases, including the death duties, and also parliamentary reform were bitter issues at the time.

Health Service Act. In the latter case the doctors themselves soon came to accept and approve what had been described as a fate worse than slavery. The Canadian family allowance system, of the same vintage, famous to Canadians as the Baby Bonus, passed with remarkable speed from the status of a shocking innovation (subsidized procreation) to the standing of an infinitely respectable and universally beloved institution.

With us, the years preceding the passage of the Social Security Act of 1935 were marked not alone by bitter resistance to the old age and survivors insurance, the unemployment compensation, and the public assistance and health and welfare services provided by the legislation, but by the most dismal of prophecies as to their consequences. Thus, prior to passage, the Senate Finance Committee considering the legislation heard that "nothing could be more certain to increase unemployment"; that it would impose a "staggering additional burden" on business firms, that many businesses would not survive the burden of social security taxes; that the legislation "raises the questions of the utmost gravity as to both the raising and safeguarding of terrifically huge sums of money"; that "when you take away from mankind the impulse to save for his [sic] own old age, you have destroyed one of the fundamental elements of human character"; that "legislation which from its very nature tends to increase dependency and indigency decreases individual energy and efficiency of individuals in attempting to take care of themselves"; and that when you "enter upon a broad policy whereby the individual is relieved of the responsibility for his unemployment, for his old age, for the care of his children, you are entering upon a pathway which has destroyed other nations. The downfall of Rome. . . ."[5]

There were reasons for expecting the American social security legislation to be peculiarly controversial. The legislation of 1935 was exceptionally comprehensive. In the years preceding we had lagged behind other industrial communities in the provision of social insurance, and we brought ourselves up to date, as it were, with a jerk. Some provisions of the law were frankly experimental, and the constitutionality of other features was in doubt.[6] Yet, long before the close of the thirties, the legislation had ceased to be controversial. No one—or very few—attacked unemployment compensation, or pensions for the aged, or public assistance for other dependent groups. Conservative fears and objections were directed not toward what

[5] *Hearings before the Committee on Finance,* United States Senate, 74th Congress, 1st Session, on S. 1130. Washington: U. S. Government Printing Office, 1935, pp. 687, 897, 941, 1104, 940, 1103.

[6] The principal provisions of the act were upheld by the Supreme Court, May 24, 1937.

existed but toward how social security might be extended. As with our neighbors, it had proved impossible to sustain a debate on the wisdom of welfare measures once these were on the statute books.

### III

An examination of the reasons why controversy over social welfare legislation collapses once it has been enacted throws useful light on the tactics of economic argument in this area. Obviously the case against any piece of welfare legislation must be based on hypothetical consequences—"assuming this legislation is passed this is what you may expect." For purposes of political suasion a bad hypothetical argument is usually as satisfactory as a good one, and it may be superior. The bad argument is no more susceptible to disproof than the good one, and it can, of course, be a great deal more dramatic. An impressive compilation of the grievous disasters which are expected to follow from the passage of the legislation will always attract more attention than something more moderate that makes sense.

Under these circumstances, there is a strong temptation to allow the imagination full rein in devising or exaggerating the consequences of legislation, and this has, indeed, become the standard tactic in opposing welfare measures. Thus, unemployment insurance was opposed on the hypothesis that the payments would be preferred to wage income. As a result, malingering would become a way of life. With only the eccentric at work, national income and output would fall, and everyone would descend into a relaxed but dismal poverty. Old age and survivors insurance was similarly attacked on the hypothesis that it would lead to total profligacy during working years, a reduction in national savings, demands for ever higher benefits, and, in the end, national bankruptcy. Other welfare legislation has been held to portend equally catastrophic prospects. It will be recalled that even restrictions on the labor of children were once held to bode the collapse of the Republic.

The unfortunate feature of this particular debating tactic is that a courageous or foolhardy public may, nonetheless, take the action which is held to be damaging. Since the consequences were synthesized for the purpose of the argument, they do not occur. The position of the opposition in the matter is forthwith discredited. As a usual result, the organization of further opposition becomes impossible. The debate comes to an end.

It follows that any individual or organization which is using the imaginative hypothetical consequence as a technique of argument should be particularly careful to see that the legislation which is opposed is never enacted into law. There is an important current lesson here for medical doctors. For some time, the American Medical Association has been picturing the hypothetical consequences of adopting a system of national health insurance. These are grim. Physicians would become puppets in a political hierarchy. There would be a prompt and gross deterioration in the standards of medical care. There would be little further progress in the art. Medical services would be monopolized by hypochondriacs. People, as distinct from politicians, would quickly come to excoriate the system, but would be caught helplessly in its toils. Soon there would be a sharp increase in death rates. Those left living would be unhealthy, unhappy, though (now) wise. As long as the American Medical Association is able to stand off such health insurance schemes, these dismal consequences will remain hypothetical and, hence, unrefuted. Should the country one day enact a health insurance scheme, there is at least a chance that medical catastrophe would not ensue. The influence of the AMA would be sadly impaired.

## IV

The fact that controversy over enacted measures subsides so quickly does not preclude a good deal of debate over measures which have not been adopted but which have been made moot by the pioneering experience of other countries or the eloquent skill of the rare political figure who is able to identify a public need and formulate a solution. For these reasons we shall continue to debate increased public aid to health, education, and improved housing, and possibly (through family allowances) to the costs of child rearing.

The debate over health insurance, one may assume, will be exceptionally sharp. Sickness, in a singular degree, renders the individual incapable of looking after himself. It remains, perhaps, the most serious of the uncertainties with which the average citizen must contend. At the same time, the opposition to health insurance stands on a different footing from that to most other welfare measures. The others—unemployment insurance, public assistance, old age and survivors insurance, workmen's compensation, aid to dependent children and to the blind—were not viewed as deeply damaging to the interests or welfare of any particular group. They were resisted on grounds of general policy, in the belief that they could not be afforded, that they were deleterious to the moral fiber of the recipients, that they reduced the will or disposition of people to work as they should, or on some similar grounds. In this argument, those with a specific interest in, say, old age pensions or unemployment compensation were pitted against those who had only their view of the general welfare (and perhaps some very modest increase in their own taxes) as their motivation to resistance. As frequently happens, those with a specific and identifiable interest prevailed.

The argument over health insurance is very different. Any state-sponsored system of prepaid med-

ical care encounters the implacable opposition of
the organized medical practitioners. This is based
on a sharp (although disputed) identification of
self-interest and long-standing conviction that the
present organization of medical care will best advance the medical art.

Here, then, those who seek the benefits of a
welfare measure face a well-organized and deter-
mined opposition. So far in this argument, moreover, it would appear that the medical profession
has had its own way. Few campaigns have been
conducted with more superficial indications of
total success than that of the doctors in recent years
against universal health insurance. It is one
indication of the extent of their victory that the
office-seeker's standard disavowal of "socialized
medicine" (the displacement of the term insurance
by the term socialism was itself a workmanlike
achievement in the technique of argument) is now
only slightly less fulsome than his disavowal of
communism.

Nevertheless, it cannot be assumed that this
argument is over. While the supporters of a national health insurance scheme would seem to
have met a decisive defeat, the problem of financing medical care for the ordinary family has
remained. This need can any time serve as culture
to a new argument. In addition, there is evidence
that social innovation, having been checked on
one medical front, is going ahead all the more

rapidly on others. This is as one would expect. The difficulty of suppressing or resisting technical innovation, no matter how unsettling or uncomfortable, has long been recognized. Even if the invention is successfully bought up and buried, another is all but certain to appear somewhere else. Though the point is not commonly recognized, the situation with social innovation is much the same. Voluntary prepayment plans for medical and hospital care have been developed as a partial alternative to more comprehensive insurance. More striking, however, is the way in which the frontal resistance to health insurance seems to have brought organized and even wholly socialized medical schemes in at the back door. Private companies have started providing medical care for their employees as part of their compensation. More significant still, in a country where most adult males and a growing number of women have seen service in the armed forces, are the rapidly expanding medical services of the Veterans Administration. While presumably intended for the veteran whose disability is connected with his service, there is inevitable elasticity in relating illness to service. Moreover, care may be had for non-service-connected disability if hospital beds are available. This is not insurance but, in effect, fully socialized medical care. Yet veterans' organizations which defend it are notably invulnerable to the charge of social radicalism.

## V

Thus the problem of organized medical care seems certain to be a continuing subject of argument. There is a somewhat similar likelihood—based on a similar juxtaposition of need to a well-organized lobby—of argument over slum clearance and public housing. There are other welfare measures, including education with its ancient but still viable dispute over segregation of church and state and non-segregation of Negroes and whites, which promise to provide some continuing fuel for controversy. Those who are repelled by the peaceful life should not be totally discouraged.

Nevertheless, the argument over the Welfare State is clearly in senile decline. As noted, the argument in the abstract—over the welfare state in general—is not viable and is unlikely to be resumed. We have noticed the tendency for argument over enacted measures to subside immediately on their becoming law, and the very good reasons why this should occur. This means that the only remaining subjects for dispute are either those like medical care, housing, and federal aid to education, which are already under discussion, or new welfare measures which are not yet an issue in the United States or have not even been invented. This latter possibility requires a moment's examination.

It is a basic tenet of the conservative faith in the United States that the ingenuity of man—or

rather of radicals—in dreaming up new social
services is endless. There is a vast reservoir of
ideas on what the government might do for the
citizen, and it is constantly being replenished by
new and ever more fantastic or, anyhow, costly
schemes. This concept of a mountainous flood of
unenacted ideas does much to explain conservative
resistance to individual items of welfare legislation. Even though the measure itself—help to
dependent children or aid to the blind—is impec-
cable in motive and moderate in cost, it must be
resisted for the reason that only by resisting any
and all such legislation can we avoid being en-
gulfed.

It seems certain that this view of the matter,
which has been singularly free from scrutiny, is
wrong. In the last fifteen years in the United
States, there have been virtually no proposals for
new social services. Those actively under debate—
housing, health, federal aid to education—have
been under debate for many years.

That the same thing seems to be true of Britain
may be even more significant. The intellectual
*avant garde* of British socialism has recently suggested that "socialists would be quite wrong to
think that the essence of socialism lies in the in-
definite extension of free service. . . . A point will
come when . . . the liberty of the citizen to spend
his income as he pleases must also be regarded."[7]

7 C. A. R. Crosland, "The Transition from Capitalism." *New
Fabian Essays,* Praeger, 1952, p. 63.

Relatively speaking, we are still well behind Britain in the development of our welfare services. The fact remains, however, that the Democrats in the United States, like the Labour party in Britain, could use some new idea of wide potential appeal on which they could campaign in the face of stalwart conservative opposition. For the moment, at least, no such idea seems to be around. The reservoir which conservatives believe so alarmingly full may, in fact, be just a mud puddle.

# SEVEN

## The Politics of Agreement and Dissent

OUR journey to the battlefields of economic controversy is now over. Not all of the scenes of conflict have been visited. The tariff, resource conservation, ownership, and development, power policy, big business, Wall Street, and monopoly are all subjects of controversy in an ancient tradition. However, labor relations and agricultural policy, the larger issues of economic management of the economy, and the questions concerning the welfare state have been, almost certainly, the most disputed economic issues of our time.

They have also been the major basis for political difference and division. Thus, in the early years of the New Deal, many individuals who supported the Republican Party did so in the confident belief that it was opposed to unions as such. Today, no sensible Republican, however heartened he might be by the complaints of the CIO, would contribute to the Republican exchequer in the hope of seeing a crushing attack on organized labor. Similarly, it was possible in the thirties to suggest that a vote

for Hoover or Landon was a vote against government intervention in agricultural markets. The
hope that this intervention might end has died
more slowly. But now it is doubtful if it will long
survive the acceptance of the inevitability of large-
scale intervention by so stalwart a conservative as
Ezra Taft Benson. It was possible to suppose that
his predecessors, but not he, preferred monkey
business for its own sake. No important issue is at
stake in the present debate on farm policy.

Twenty years ago—or for that matter ten years
ago—nothing was better calculated to produce a
coronary occlusion in the American right than the
suggestion that the American economy should be
managed, or could be managed, from Washington.
This was the quintessence of New Deal nonsense—
or cupidity. Within the past year, urged by the
apparent threat of a depression, a Republican
president has said: "Government must be alert and
sensitive to economic developments. . . . It must be
prepared to take preventive as well as remedial
action; and it must be prepared to cope with new
situations that may arise."[1] As between the two
major parties the principle of government responsibility for a high level of employment and output
in the economy is no longer an issue. A debate will

[1] *Economic Report of the President,* transmitted to the Congress of the United States, January 28, 1954. 83rd Congress. 2nd
Session. Washington: U. S. Government Printing Office, 1954,
p. iv.

continue, but it will be on the method, vigor, and timing of such intervention.

We have just seen that the general issue of the welfare state is not a vital subject of controversy. On individual welfare measures not only does action foreclose dispute, but there is at least a chance that more of the debate is in the past than in the future.

In brief, none of the great questions of economic policy which provided such rich fuel for political controversy in the thirties and the forties now retains its old standing as a subject of disagreement. The political parties have come to share the same strategic goals and to divide only on tactics.

For an argument that invokes a major issue of principle, in fact, it is necessary to go back to such questions as the tariff and the related matters of trade policy. It is interesting that, as a subject of argument, this issue should have so much more vitality and durability than those brought to the forefront by the New and Fair Deals. As for a hundred and fifty years, there continues to be a deep division between those who identify their interest, and that of the country at large, with low tariffs and liberal trade, and those who fix their eyes on the advantages of relieving a domestic industry—their own, that of their community, or congressional district—from the inconveniences of foreign competition. There is a fundamental difference here. There is no common ground between the man who believes in low tariffs or free trade, large imports, and who assumes participation in a larger world economy, and the man who confines his view to the advantage of a particular firm or industry. There is no compromise between the advocates of more trade and the advocates of less trade that can be pleasing to both. This is a disagreement in principle.

There is an important practical lesson here. Because most economic argument in our time is over questions of tactics or method, we are disposed to be optimistic about our ability to reach an acceptable agreement on most issues that arise. However, no one should be blind to the existence of the limiting case of disagreement on principle where compromise is not possible and where it should not be sought. Thus, in the winter of 1953-54, the Chairman of the President's Commission on Foreign Economic Policy, Mr. Clarence B. Randall, and his low-tariff colleagues sought to find a basis of agreement on the issue of trade and tariff policy with such redoubtable exponents of protection as Senator Eugene D. Millikin and Representatives Daniel A. Reed and Richard M. Simpson. This was inherently impossible and should not have been tried. The results were decidedly unfortunate. Concessions were made to the protectionists—rather more than were wise. But since the principle of protection itself was not conceded, these concessions were insufficient to win agreement.

The argument over the tariff shows again the extent to which we are traditionalists in economic controversy, the extent to which we prefer not the new rows but the old. On the new rows—those that made the air and the air waves hideous in the days of the New and Fair Deals—we are in an era of extending rather than narrowing agreement. What are the consequences of this extraordinary and seemingly so unnatural amiability?

## II

First, one major qualification to the foregoing trend to agreement must be noted. The agreement here being discussed is not between individuals but between organizations and specifically between the two major political parties. One always needs to inquire how fully any particular organization reflects the concensus of its members. The existence of a sizeable dissident minority is obviously of interest and importance. During the thirties and forties, the Democratic party was, as a party, committed to the general body of New and Fair Deal legislation. But many members of the Democratic party—the conservative southern Democrats in particular—were anything but committed. The Southerners also regarded themselves, not without reason, as the natural and traditional spokesmen of their party.

Among its purposes, a political party has that of making effective the ideas of the individuals who belong to it. Men join parties (among other reasons) to get an amplified voice for their ideas and to see their ideas translated into action. This being so, there are obvious grounds for irritation, annoyance, and frustration when the party advocates ideas the opposite of those for which the individual seeks a voice. Frustration is certain if the individual must support a party in opposition to his own views because he has no alternative.

This, in some measure, was the position of the conservative southern Democrat during much of the period from 1932 to 1952. He belonged to a party which advanced ideas antithetical to his own. For reasons deep in our history, he had no easy alternative, although the formation of the States Rights party in 1948 and the defection to Eisenhower in 1952 showed that something could be done.

There is a potentially more serious source of frustration in the present state of political agreement. While both parties accept collective bargaining, farm price supports, a positive government economic policy, and the social welfare legislation which comprises the welfare state, there are many individuals who do not. These things are still anathema to the powerful right wing of the Republican party in Congress, to numerous conservatives of both parties throughout the country, including many exceedingly solvent Texans, and to a highly articulate corps of columnists, commentators, and followers of Colonel Robert R. McCormick.

The usual mark of those who take an extreme position is that they feel strongly about it; were it otherwise they would already have modified their position by compromise. Those who are against unions and farm price supports and government responsibility for economic performance and the welfare state are likely to be uncompromisingly against these things. Most of them are Republicans, and, like the southern Democrats of yore, they feel that they are the natural custodians of the traditions of their party. It is in this frame of mind that they contemplate the acceptance of a nearly opposite position by an administration which is also Republican.

The position of the Executive in this matter should be carefully understood. It is a position that derives much less from choice than from necessity. One of the persistent, indeed, all but universal, errors in our view of political life lies in the respective roles assigned to ideology and to circumstance. It is assumed, as a matter of course, that an administration in Washington has a wide range of choice of policy and action depending on whether it wishes to be radical or conservative, wise or obtuse. In reality, the opportunity for such choice is small. A strenuously reformist administration, like that of early New Deal, can provide itself with some range of ideological choice. But most administrations (this was true of Truman's, and it is evidently even more true of Eisenhower's) are in David Riesman's invaluable phrase "other-directed."[2] Given the circumstances, a knowledge of popular attitudes, and a desire for re-election, the action, Democratic or Republican, will be much the same. It is an article of faith of the Republican right that the Eisenhower administration took over the domestic and foreign policies of Truman, that it deliberately adopted a "Me-Too" formula. In point of fact, it was controlled by the same circumstances that controlled its predecessor. (It is perhaps part of the political genius of Democrats that they are more adept than Republicans in taking credit for the inevitable.) Perhaps the point can be most clearly perceived in relation to policies in countering depression. There is a widespread notion that one of the most primitive of modern ideological choices is whether a government shall be Keynesian or not. In fact, faced with the reality of a depression, this comes to nothing more or less than a choice of whether or not to commit political suicide. Abetted by a strongly traditional view of government finance—a deep indoctrination of fiscal sanity —a strong president like Mr. Hoover was able to exercise the choice in favor of suicide. He was

[2] David Riesman, Nathan Glazer, and Reuel Denney, *The Lonely Crowd*. New York: Doubleday Anchor, 1953.

probably the last to whom this opportunity was open. No present or future administration really has the non-Keynesian choice, come a serious depression, of trying to balance the budget and letting nature, unemployment, farm prices, and the Democrats all take their course.

It follows that there is a basic source of division in political life between those who have responsibility for consequences and those who do not. The man who is under the day-to-day pressure of circumstances adjusts his ideas accordingly. Such an adjustment is commonplace in the federal Executive quite without regard to the ideological point of departure. By contrast, the man who is not under the pressure of circumstances retains his ideological freedom. This is the happy situation of the Congressman and Senator, columnist and commentator. Under almost any conditions we should expect this difference in the disciplining role of circumstance and responsibility to be a cause of trouble between Executive and Congress.

## III

To a quite extraordinary degree, politico-economic argument in our day is dominated by the protests of those who have been left outside the general concensus on principle. These—the men who do not accept the general agreement on unions, farm prices, economic management, and welfare—are our political displaced persons. In addition to their congressional representation they have a marked influence on press and radio and possess also the peculiar strength which arises from the righteous conviction that only what is traditional is truly American. Much of the political machinery of the Republican party is in their hands. Many believed they won in the 1952 election. But any real hope of achieving their program is denied them. As a result, these dissidents are reduced almost entirely to guerrilla warfare. They cannot advance the principles in which they believe; they can only harass the massive forces they oppose. They can, as in the recent Congress, resist the President on housing legislation, or in amending the Taft-Hartley Act, or on like matters. They have no hope of repealing the legislation they oppose.

We have here the explanation of the peculiar vigor of the economic protest which comes, in these days, from the extreme right. We have been accustomed, for many years, to extreme language from the left—to violent denunciation of the exploiters of the poor, angry slogans about release from the chains. Such shrill techniques of argument are, it is reasonably certain, the by-product of frustration. This was so when they were used on the left. It is so now that they are used on the right.

And the cause is clear. The man who sees a chance for accomplishing his aims seeks to win friends. He is persuasive, well-mannered, and ingratiating, and, in the end, disposed to a reasonable compromise. The man who sees no hope for his ideas need make no such concessions to amiable behavior. He can be polemical, unreasonable, self-righteous, and violent, for it makes no difference. Since the knowledge that his ideas have no chance is not likely to put him in a good temper, the likelihood of violent behavior is doubtless increased.

I began this essay with a reference to the strong language and angry denunciation which characterize so much of our political debate. We are now in a position to understand them, and on few subjects is misunderstanding so easy. Much of our debate is loud and violent, not because the issues are close but because they are not. There is anger not because issues are being settled but because they are settled. The noise, nonetheless, leaves the impression that the matter is still in doubt. Although a vehement argument may mean that an important question is being decided, it far more frequently means only that a hopelessly outnumbered minority is making itself felt in the only way it can.

## IV

I have cited this problem of the displaced minority as a problem of the Republicans. This must not be thought partisan; the Republicans' misfortune in this matter is that they are the more conservative of the two major parties. The more liberal, or, more precisely, the politically more aggressive Democrats, staked out the advanced position on the issues here under discussion. (While doing so they had their troubles with *their* conservative wing.) The Republicans, all the while in opposition, had no need to take a categorical position on the economic issues which the New and Fair Deals had raised. Some members of the party could go along; others could object. None had to assume responsibility. When the quadrennial conventions arrived, disputes in the Resolutions Committee could be composed by a form of words.

With the assumption of power, the years of this agreeable finesse came to an end. The resulting split in the Republican party is, without doubt, a serious one. No one should too readily conclude, however, that is final. Our parties split far more often in principle than in practice. The danger of division always seems acute; the fatal divisions, like those of the Republicans in 1912, are rare. As a healing salve, the desire to hold office has, in our system, the standing of a miracle drug.

Moreover, in the present case, time works on the side of repair. It is the present misfortune of the Republicans that the Democrats, in the thirties, staked out positions which the conservative minority still rejects. Had the Democrats been passive or had they been able to be passive in face of circumstances, the Republicans would not now be in trouble. But the Democrats have staked out little new ground in the last ten years; the idea-breeding, which created such a ferment in the thirties, came to an end with the war, and no one has seriously accused the Democratic party of having a new or dangerous thought for fifteen years. Thus, for the time being, no new problems of accommodation are being created. Meanwhile, as time passes, there are fewer and fewer Republicans with memories of the doctrines and delights of the age of William McKinley or even of Calvin Coolidge. There are more and more who see compromise on economic issues as common sense rather than as historical betrayal. It is conceivable that some man, charged like Colonel Robert R. McCormick with the true spirit of Don Quixote, but younger, might undertake to lead the truly uncompromising conservatives out of the Republican party. But this danger, like the danger that the latter might seize the party, is small and diminishing. It is only the capacity of the dissidents in the short run to disrupt and to immobilize the Republican party which should not be underestimated.

## V

Let me now return, however, to the larger agreement on principle which is the more important conclusion of this essay. I shall not pause to inquire whether this agreement is a good thing. It is part of our genius as a people—or anyhow part of our ingenuity—to discover equal virtue, or, on occasion, equal vice, in exact opposites. Of the venting of the most reeking billingsgate we say that it is vigorous argument in the best two-fisted American tradition. When two antagonists suddenly withdraw their thumbs from each other's eyes, we say it is compromise in the best American tradition of burying the hatchet. We may conclude that both the past contention on economic matters and the present amiability are good. Both bring out the better points of our national character.

However, there is one consequence which is worth noting. At any given time, it seems probable that the element of faction in our political life is approximately a constant. Certain numbers of our political figures always achieve their distinction by being negotiators, brokers, and architects of compromise. These are the men, the Warrens, and Vandenburgs, and Rayburns, and Barclays, who do not have to pick battles to sustain themselves in the public eye. But the more typical political career requires controversy; political recognition or notoriety is won by participation in argument and dispute. If such a politician cannot argue over one thing, then he must quick a quarrel over something else. If he cannot condemn the Welfare State, then he must attack the British. It follows that our political system, and the large premium which it places on free political enterprise, requires that there be a given minimum controversy at any given time. Should it ever develop that there are no real grounds of dispute at any moment, some must be invented. Peace for one genus of politician means political destruction.

The argument which is selected by the political controversialist at any time is likely to reflect in a tolerably accurate way the underlying urgency of the issues. During the thirties the fact of depression, plus the genuine questions of principle which were at stake in economic controversy, made economic matters the central focus of debate. It was here, more than incidentally, that the demagogues also operated. Huey Long's preoccupation with foreign policy was minimal; he unerringly concentrated on economics.

For the same reason, economic controversy has dropped to a lesser, if not precisely secondary, position in our time. Problems of foreign policy are far more ardently debated. Europe and Asia at the moment occupy the energies that were once concentrated on deposit insurance and the free coinage of silver. Likewise in our time, the pathological controversialists have deserted economics to prey upon the doubt, uncertainty, and insecurity which we encounter when we look abroad. His personal finances apart, Senator McCarthy has never shown much interest in economic questions, although, it must be added, with no serious loss to the subject matter. The demagogue is never irrelevant. Nothing might serve us better

than some convenient economic disorder which
would bring our pathological controversialists back
from foreign policy in the atomic age to something
relatively safe.

## VI

Enough has been said to suggest that controversy
on economics, as on other matters, has a dynamic
of its own. It is capable of developing an intensity
which is unrelated to issues. Indeed, the intensity of the debate may be inversely related to the
urgency of the questions involved. None of this
is easily seen. Those of us who are most concerned
with controversy are most disposed to participate.
The battle line is a poor place from which to view
the battle. We should, on occasion, get a larger
perspective on the melee and on the weapons,
tactics, and objectives. So viewed, some of the
battles will doubtless be shown to be very important. Some, it will be found, are being fought with
blank cartridges for ground that has already been
won in a war that is over.

# Index

P2b,82